Marianne Grabrucker, born 1948, is a federal judge in Germany and worked for five years as head of the local Commission for Women. She has published various books, especially on the law and women.

D0244862

0075504

THERE'S A GOOD GIRL

GENDER STEREOTYPING IN THE FIRST THREE YEARS OF LIFE: A DIARY

With a new afterword by the author and her daughter, translated by Tiffany Cummings

MARIANNE GRABRUCKER

TRANSLATED BY WENDY PHILIPSON

0075504

301·185.14 GRA

First published in English by The Women's Press Ltd, 1988
A member of the Namara Group
34 Great Sutton Street, London EC1V 0DX

Reprinted with new material 1995

First published in Germany as *Typisch Mädchen: Praegung
in den ersten drei Lebensjahren – ein Tagebuch* by S Fischer
Verlag, Frankfurt am Main

Copyright © Marianne Grabrucker 1988, 1995
Translation copyright © Wendy Philipson 1988
Afterword translation copyright © Tiffany Cummings 1995

The right of Marianne Grabrucker to be identified as the
author of this work has been asserted by her in accordance
with the Copyright, Designs and Patents Act 1988.

British Library Cataloguing-in-Publication Data
Grabrucker, Marianne
  There's a good girl: gender stereotyping in the first three
  years of life, a diary.
  1. Infant psychology   2. Self-perception in children
  I. Title   II. Typisch Mädchen. *English*
  115.4'22   BF720.S44

This book is sold subject to the condition that it shall not,
by way of trade or otherwise, be lent, re-sold, hired out, or
otherwise circulated without the Publisher's prior consent
in any form of binding or cover other than that in which it
is published and without a similar condition including this
condition being imposed on the subsequent purchaser.

ISBN 0 7043 4090 9

Typeset in Times by Contour Typesetters, Southall, London
Printed and bound in Great Britain by
BPC Paperbacks, Aylesbury, Bucks

Contents

Contents

Introduction

A child is born, a new woman has arrived. And her future is going to be different.

These were more or less the thoughts that I and women friends and acquaintances had when my daughter was born. It was like starting school, the New Year, a new job or a new love affair; it was all going to be different this time – better. I was going to avoid all the old mistakes, or at least those we thought we understood. I would be cautious and diplomatic, would employ tact and the right sense of balance, so that a 'new woman' could unfold naturally.

I was, of course, simply following relevant theories of social conditioning, proceeding on the assumption that it is education which forms man and woman.[1] For my daughter things were going to be different. She was not going to become like us, that is, women who were born in the post-war period. I did not want her to accept from her male contemporaries what we had accepted as regards education, work and personal relationships. I did not want her to be compliant, to keep her opinions to herself and to smile sweetly instead of contradicting. I did not want her to be always checking and rethinking her ideas before daring to open her mouth, unlike her male counterparts who would say everything three times and then repeat it once again. And I did not want her to be completely devoted to some man who would be continually finding fault with and criticising her until she lost faith in herself. I wanted her to avoid having plans for the future which were modest and which fitted in neatly with the reality of women's lives. My daughter was going to reach for the stars!

The theory was that our generation and the thousands of generations of women before us had been prevented from achieving all these things by a process of gender conditioning determined by centuries of patriarchy. This process had to be broken. My daughter's socialisation was going to be different – this was to be a new start and traditional influences were going to be eliminated as far as possible. I myself was determined to make no mistakes in this respect and I really believed that I was capable of this. I thought that my involvement and growth in the second wave of the women's movement in the late sixties, my own experience of personal relationships and of discrimination in my studies and in my profession as a lawyer had made me proof against any risk of my bringing up a child to be a typical girl. I had thought and talked about it too much to believe myself susceptible to that. If everything were caused by education then everything could equally well be avoided through education – such was the conclusion I came to.

There was, however, no place in my schema for a girl who was a good chap. I did not want that either. I painted myself a picture of a human being who had not been forced into adopting any gender role, according to standard patterns of male or female, but who would unfold and develop free of stereotypes. There had been many Summerhills, but I felt that in all such experiments one aspect had been given too little attention: the main concern had been with *man*kind, whilst womankind had been lost and forgotten.

I kept a diary about the development of my daughter. In the course of time I grew less sure and began to doubt my premises. I was often on the point of abandoning my theories and accepting a belief in innate gender-specific behaviour, for so many 'feminine' aspects of my daughter's behaviour could not possibly have been learned from me. And I was confirmed in this by many critical and emancipated mothers who were absolutely convinced that they were bringing up their children in a manner free of gender prejudice. For they too seemed to find, especially if they had both a daughter and a son, that there really were innate boy and girl traits. Nothing could be done about this, it simply had to be accepted. We shared many a sigh. But the mothers of boys seemed less concerned than the mothers of girls. One woman, who had written a master's dissertation on this subject and had had a son in the meantime, put it like this: 'I've abandoned all my theories and accept the fact that there really is an innate difference.' The idea was even beginning to find favour in feminist writings and to gain ground.[2]

Though not explicitly, these opinions seem to me to accept that education by the mother is the decisive factor in overcoming the restrictive gender role in girls. Such a belief has become fixed in the minds of the present generation of mothers. It had grown since 1968 along with the new women's movement in the course of which gender role behaviour had once again become problematical. One thing stuck in the heads of women:

We have made ourselves fully aware how ideology is passed from generation to generation and how it can survive all material realities: through education, handed on ironically almost exclusively by just those oppressed beings who have most urgent need of liberation: women ... Who then is supposed to be responsible for this new education? – Well, there can be only one answer to that: since the system makes use of women to hand down images of themselves, then women must make use of the system to overcome it! . . . So we stick with the theory that education is a means to emancipation.[3]

Other academic positions and insights which considered the whole social complex[4] were not taken into account by the majority of women and remained within the category of specialist literature. We insisted on the dominance of education, riddled though it was with the complexes of a Freudian nature we had long become accustomed to.

Inwardly I began to resist this. This maternal fatalism! This submission to fate! At the end of each day I began to make a precise account of everything that had happened, what I had said and done and what had been passed on to Anneli and her male and female friends – always from the point of view of what part these trivial, often insignificant, events might play in role creating. My sensitivity grew in direct ratio to my understanding. Days teemed with role-enforcing events, concealed and obvious, for which I was only rarely responsible.

An accumulation of such experiences provides the child with a pattern, in accordance with which it is bound to adjust its own behaviour within its environment. Only when I had gained this general view from three years of observing quite chance events, and grasped all the details as part of a whole picture, did I realise that I and the world around were building brick by brick a woman governed by patriarchy, and not a human being with female or male components. And so much of this happened unconsciously, unintentionally, without reflection or real understanding of the situation. For these reasons the mothers I spoke to about it denied that their approach to their children's upbringing was gender differentiated, as I would also no doubt have done without the diary. For the first time I recognised many things in everyday life as being gender stereotyped and realised that everything happened like a computer program set to 'girl upbringing'.

I am therefore now convinced that mothers who proceed from a belief in the innate differences in behaviour of the sexes are falling victim to a mechanism which keeps on reproducing itself. Behaviour patterns are handed on unconsciously. The result is then labelled 'innate' and it is here that the mistake is made. I therefore think it both mistaken and dangerous when progressive and thoughtful mothers begin to believe that there are innate differences just because, despite the best of intentions, they themselves are having no apparent success in rearing their children differently from traditional patterns.

It is the many tiny events that create a total picture, and at the end of it all we stand amazed at our typical 'girl' or 'boy'. It is also clear that it takes more than simply giving a boy a doll to make a girl of him. That is achieved only by the sum of all influences over a long period of time, of years. It cannot be over-emphasised that it is not only mothers trying to bring up their children in an emancipated fashion who influence their children, but that the young grow up in an 'atmosphere' which without any doubt favours one sex.

In a male-oriented society all conditions are better for bringing up boys rather than girls. This is no hollow assertion. I felt that the daily preoccupation with events helped me to begin to understand this 'atmosphere'. Everybody denies that they make any distinction in the rearing of girls and boys. Boys also have to help in the house, mothers assure me; they have to do the dusting and by the age of four they are already able to make the coffee. This is all stressed as being particularly progressive, and pronounced with suitable emphasis and applause for the boy! Of course he gets a doll; of course he can cry! Such mothers would never say to their sons 'boys don't cry'. Nowadays it is taken for granted that girls run around in trousers, play just as wildly, get dirty and have the same toys as boys. Everybody is aware that there is such a thing as gender specific upbringing – but it is happening somewhere else, in other, more conservative, families. Perhaps with mothers with a traditional image of the world which has never become confused or been questioned, somewhere else anyway, not in our family. Later on, when the children go to kindergarten or school, we are aware from our reading of relevant literature that there is gender specific education and that we shall have to react against it at home. But until then, as long as we have the rearing of our children in our own hands, there are no differences. The very worst that can happen is that we might reject the idea of sending a boy to ballet classes or perhaps allow a girl to wear a dress instead of trousers on a hot summer's day. But that's all, we would swear to it.

We were therefore rather dismayed to read Elena Gianini Belotti on conventional parental behaviour. We cannot believe that the examples she quotes in her book, *Little Girls*, which appeared in Italy in 1973 and is based on Italian educational practices, could be relevant to the situation in the Federal Republic of Germany in the 1980s. Our opinion is shared by the publishing collective, Women's Offensive, and by Ilse Brehmer who writes in an essay on feminist pedagogics:

> Many of the results quoted seem dubious (for example, that mothers in general give less attention to daughters during breast feeding, that pink clothing for girls has some special meaning). Some of the results were based on laboratory experiments in America and France. Few general conclusions can be drawn from results achieved in such an artificial framework, and other observations are probably significant only within specific cultures. All other things have probably become outdated because of the developments of recent years, in particular the renewed women's movement. More detailed investigations and inter-cultural comparisons are needed here.[6]

We therefore do not feel that most of this research has any relevance for us. Deluded by the fact that there are no empirically proven points on the question of gender stereotyping in the FRG we conclude that it does not exist here, or at least not in this form. So many things have changed, we say. Gender stereotyping is not true of people like us, fairly progressive, politically aware individuals.

Moreover, there are no detailed studies relating to the first three years of life, based on the experiences of a small child in the private world of the family.[7] The treatment of children is not public until they start to go to playgroup.[8]

All the adults who had any part in the making of this book are open-minded, liberal people, some of them politically active and like myself members of the 1968 generation, who want to bring up their children to be free of the chains of gender. Their goal in education, they say, is to encourage self-confidence, pleasure in decision-making, an ability to hold one's own, critical insight and sensitivity.

But then it all turns out quite differently – as this diary has shown me, and will, I hope, show other mothers of both girls and boys. It will, it is to be hoped, be a signal to all parents and, above all, to those who like myself reject the idea of conscious gender stereotyping in their children's upbringing.

The events described here happened principally in Berlin and Munich. Our home is in Munich and there Anneli lived in the father–mother–child nuclear family, where her father earned the money and was away from home from Monday to Friday and was available only in the evenings and at weekends. Since I was not earning and had more freedom I took the opportunity to visit friends and family in Berlin quite often, and there Anneli lived in the society of emancipated feminist women, with me but without her father. We also spent some time each year in the nearby Alps, in villages in the Tyrol or Switzerland. Anneli was thus exposed to a wide spectrum of behaviour and attitudes, between the progressive north and the ultra conservative south.*

Of course, the scenes described here form only one part of Anneli's early life. It would be possible to write a similar diary about a child growing up in our society referring to other

---

*The north has always felt itself to be politically far in advance of the agricultural south. Even today, Berlin feminists are inclined to consider that the women of Bavaria lag behind. In the agricultural areas of the South Tyrol traditional opinions regarding women are still predominant. (*Translator's note.*)

processes, cleanliness, for example. Aspects of my daughter's sexuality are not included, although they were in my original notes; the subject and the conclusions are so extensive that they need a book of their own.

Munich 1985

The response to my diary has made it clear how great the interest in its themes is; in Germany the first edition sold out in less than two months, and it has now sold over 100,000 copies, and been translated into Finnish, as well as English. It is a standard text in German universities, on women's studies, psychology and pedagogics courses. It was widely and encouragingly reviewed and since the diary first appeared many groups of women (students, young mothers, teachers) have contacted me with support, questions or a request that I should speak with them.

Of course, there have been a few critical responses. I have been taken to task for not providing a better planned, more energetic and decisive intervention in her upbringing; for presenting myself as a passive, housewifely model to my daughter, for not writing more of her father's (Klaus's) part in her upbringing. But the diary was, as well as a record of some of Anneli's experiences as I saw them, an account of learning processes of my own; I do not believe I have minimised my own shortcomings, but in the course of writing and learning over three years, I have become more aware of the effect of my own part in the story and I have tried to correct and improve it. Much that influenced Anneli was in any case beyond my control. I recorded Klaus's part in the story when it appeared to me relevant, but only he could write about his feelings, opinions and reactions. Some people regretted not finding a prescription for gender-neutral child rearing in the book, but this, of course, was never my intention. Only when we have pooled and shared our experiences and opinions might we come closer to this.

The overwhelming response to the book has been positive and hundreds of women have written, both humorously and in anger, confirming my experiences with examples from both their own and their children's upbringing. One of the more positive effects has been a modification of approach to children's play in many playgroups, at least locally, and a desire to give greater support to little girls.

I was both surprised and grateful to The Women's Press for making the diary available in English for the first time in 1988. There are no doubt differences in methods of bringing up children in Great Britain but not so great, I believe, as to make my experiences unfamiliar. I am now very pleased to see a revised edition appear, some ten years after I completed my diary. My new afterword includes a commentary from Anneli, enabling us both to assess the longer-term benefits of my approach to her upbringing. I hope a lot more women enjoy reading the book.

Munich 1994

Notes

1 Ursula Scheu, 1981.
2 cf. Anna Erler, 1983, p 91ff.; Barbara Sictermann, in *6th Youth Report*, p 24.
3 Antje Kuntsmann, 1971, pp. 119, 129, 131.
4 e.g. P.H. Mussen, 1978; Lawrence Kohlberg, 1984.
5 cf. Dagmar Schultz, 1980; Gabriele Karsten, 1977; Senta Trömel-Plötz, 1984.
6 Luise Pusch, 1983, p 370.
7 cf. Bundestag, *6th Youth Report*, 1984, p 24; Ursula Scheu, 1981, p 16.
8 Christa Preissing and Edetraud Best in *6th Youth Report*, 1984, p 24.

The Diary

March 1981 (fourth month of pregnancy)
After the amniocentesis I learn that my baby is a girl.

I have the feeling that I only have to take the finished picture, the completely formed figure of the girl inside me, out of the drawer. She has already been born, for my imagination has created her: a beautiful, strong, self-confident, lively and intelligent creature. All the qualities she will, in my opinion, need and must have in order to be happy and successful in this masculine society.

Klaus, on the other hand, pictures a sweet and cuddly little girl who will love to snuggle up to him.

1981 (pregnancy)
There are some women who do not get spots and blemishes and stretch marks during pregnancy, who do not put on too much weight, but are simply beautiful. I'm one of them and I'm feeling beautiful. For the first time in my life I feel all round – in the best sense of the word – satisfaction with my appearance.

I order some expensive silk dresses, I buy myself marvellous wide silk blouses and I revel in luxury. Although I know there is absolutely no rational reason for it I am inspired by the idea that with her inside me my beauty is her beauty, too. I want to look as beautiful as possible, just for *her*, and yet at the same time I feel it is *she* who is making me beautiful. I feel a sense of complete identification with my daughter and this is expressed in our beauty. If she were a boy all this would be unthinkable.

I talked to some other pregnant women, who also already know the sex of their child, about our ideas and feelings regarding the sex of our children. Those who are expecting daughters see the child as a repetition of themselves; they feel a strong sense of attachment to their daughters and also feel quite competent to care for them until well after puberty. They know what it's like. They envisage a better future for their daughters.

Those who are expecting boys say that above all the son binds them more closely to their father and their love for him. Otherwise they feel some uncertainty about their male foetuses and cannot envisage their future. They just want to wait and see how things turn out and then adapt to the 'character' of the child. Nothing is preordained by the mother. She does not have any idea of a better life for him at the back of her mind, nor can she have, because she is not familiar with the problems a boy has in growing up. He is different from his mother, and this difference creates distance. Paula, whose second child was a girl, says

> 'I'm glad my first child was a boy. That was the right thing for me then. When I had my first child I hadn't really come to terms with myself, didn't understand my role as a woman. The way I saw myself then, I wouldn't have had the right approach with a daughter; I found it much easier with a son, because that was quite new and different. I didn't need to sort myself out in the same way.'

Paula seems to me to be expressing something that is essential in women's attitudes to their daughters. There are three important points:

1. The mother identifies completely with her daughter. What she herself has experienced as a woman is going to be valid for her daughter, too. The mother faces her daughter confidently and communicates her role as a woman to the small girl. The rules for her upbringing have been worked out by the mother from her own experience and she is familiar with them.
2. She works out an image which is quite different from the traditional one of women. Only with this confidence of the 'new woman' does she feel able to face her daughter. The girl is then confronted with this new image.
3. With a boy the approach is quite different – just because of that little appendage dangling between his legs and all the fantasies that go with it. The mother has quite different rules for him from the

ones she applies to herself. He's fixed as 'the other' and is part of a continuity; here there is no need of a 'new woman'. Perhaps the mother's very insecurity as regards her son makes her secure, since in this respect she is at least socially at one with the general sexual hierarchy.

19 August 1981 (birth)
When I see her for the first time, when I look into her face and she into my eyes – she's lying on my stomach and the umbilical cord has just been cut – I think: 'She's beautiful, she has well proportioned features, she's pretty.' And I'm overwhelmed with relief and think 'Well, that'll make things a bit easier for her.' Because I've learned from personal experience that a woman has to look good to justify her existence in this world. Only then has she any right to open her mouth, to make demands without being laughed at (more than otherwise), is permitted to have wishes and to be choosy, not just making do with what happens to come her way. She can expect things of men, because she's got something to offer. Above all in the choice of partner. I'm full of vague fears for my daughter and worry that she will, after all, end up dependent on some man, on the benevolence and understanding of one partner, and I'm afraid things will only turn out okay if she can make her choice and not make do with second best.

These are all my own fears and problems I thought I'd got over long ago but which are now resurfacing. Apparently such anxieties, in the best patriarchal tradition, were latent; deep down I'm ready to pass them on to the next generation.

25 August 1981 (6 days old)
In the street we bump into a young doctor acquaintance of ours whose critical approach to traditional medicine had earned my respect. When Klaus tells him of Anneli's birth he says 'Well, congratulations all the same old chap!' and gives Klaus a commiserating slap on the back. At first I don't quite understand, then I feel hurt and humiliated and for a fraction of a second it's as though my daughter were nothing, or at least quite easily to be disregarded.

I wonder whether newborn infants can sense such reactions? I hope she's less sensitive than Leboyer says small babies are.

November 1981 (3 months)

waiting at the doctor's with a friend who's bringing her second child – a son – for his first check-up. Her first child is a girl.

This pediatrician is *the* in-doctor in Munich. He's called in to all the best home deliveries and everyone raves about how good he is with children.

The door opens, the doctor comes in and beams at Uschi. 'Well, congratulations. No problems, were there? Isn't it a great feeling for a woman to have given life to a man?'

I'm standing next to her, with nothing more to my credit than a daughter, like Uschi herself until now.

He was the doctor who first examined Anneli after she had been born at home. I now begin to wonder whether he does in fact treat all newborn babies the same.

Winter 1981–82 (3 to 7 months)
I regularly meet one of my women colleagues, a lawyer, who had a son three weeks after I had Anneli.

Every time we meet, Karin admires Anneli, saying how pretty she is, how dainty and graceful her legs are, and what a good ballet dancer she'd make. She admires Anneli's long eyelashes and blue eyes and says that later on her flirtatious glance, her smile and delicate figure will turn men's heads and they'll run after her. 'Anneli will be able to twist men round her little finger,' she says.

But neither his mother nor I say anything like this about her son. Neither of us paints a picture of a future geared to his appearance or of his market value with women. In his case we are amused when he pees in a wide arc as his nappy is being changed, or we just talk about his eating and sleeping habits.

Later I discuss this with Uschi, the mother of one-year-old Annalena, and she has a similar tale to tell. During a visit to a friend who has a son they talk first about how adorable Annalena looks – this is their main topic of conversation – and then about the boy's abilities, his progress and development.

Then I suddenly remember Margaret Mead, who said that a girl was important to the tribe, or society, by her very existence, because of her reproductive function; she doesn't need to achieve anything to justify herself, as men and boys do.[1] Is this what's at the bottom of our behaviour? A girl is admired simply because she exists, because of her beauty, but a boy has to do something more than simply be there to attract attention; he has to define himself by playing with objects and by acquiring skills.

August 1982 (1 year)

Quite often recently I've noticed Anneli playing with her vagina, or sitting naked on the big teddy bear wriggling around on it with obvious pleasure. She is clearly aware of and interested in sexual responses.

When I can escape from house and child I go into an academic bookshop to look through books on the development of small female children. There are shelves crammed full of books on bringing up children. None of them is about 'how to raise girls'. That at least no longer has a place in modern pedagogics. Thank goodness.

I dip into some of the books and decide that my criterion for selecting one to buy will be apropos the chapter on sexuality. It's relevant right now, after all.

But, surprise, surprise. In all the books there are long discourses on sexuality – in boys. The penis forms a central point, and grouped around it is everything Freud and his successors have had to say on the topic. And then in one book I discover the following sentence: 'the development in female babies and small children follows a similar pattern'.

Where girls get a mention they're simply compared to boys. Never the other way round. Boys are the norm. Couldn't such literature give parents the impression that girls have no sexuality of their own? Isn't that what not acknowledging, not expressing, really says? So that observations of anything different in one's own child may give rise to anxiety, to the assumption that there's something wrong – observations that may at best be ignored, but rarely accepted for what they really are.

Are girls asexual creatures then? Who feel no desire?

6 December 1982 (16 months)

It's St Nicholas' Day.* Four children are together, waiting, two

---

*Traditionally, on 6 December in Germany a person dressed as St Nicholas (possibly with his assistant, Grampus) comes and asks children how they've behaved over the past year. 'Good' children are 'rewarded' and 'naughty' ones are 'punished'. In practice they usually all get toys and sweets. (*Translator's note.*)

girls and two boys. Although there are only a few weeks' difference in age, the children have reached different stages in their
development. Erich is the least bright; he grasps things slowly and
is not very sensitive. St Nicholas comes into the room. We adults
sing a carol. Three of the children sit quietly and watch what's
happening. But not Erich. He's the only one who takes absolutely
no notice of what is going on around him and runs about prattling
on as before. His little sack of goodies has to be forced on him by
his mother. None of the children shows any sign of fear.

When it's all over the adults discuss it and Erich's mother says:
'Well, my son showed the most spirit. That boy isn't afraid of anything, the way he was running around St Nicholas.'

I'm amazed at the way Erich's mother ignores the truth. How
simply and quickly a boy's mother can interpret lack of compre-
hension and sensitivity as manliness and strength. In the case of a
girl it would have been 'She doesn't understand yet.'

Anneli has got a toy lorry from St Nicholas. But the two boys
play with it, not Anneli. And when Klaus tries to interest her in it
the next day she's still not keen. I don't know why. But I'm not
interested in the lorry, either, and I don't play with it with her.
Beyond their function as a means of transport cars have no attrac-
tion for me. So I simply reject them as toys for my daughter.

20 December 1982 (16 months)

Friends of ours who have a three-year-old son are visiting us. The
boy is looking at a book with beautiful pictures of animals in it. On
one page there's a picture of a grouse hen and cock. The child asks
why the two birds look so different from one another. His father
says, 'Well, that's because one of the birds is the husband and the
other's the wife. And nature has arranged things so that the husband is always brighter and more beautiful than the wife. The
wives are always grey and plain. Just like human beings.'

His son gazes at him wide-eyed, credulous and earnest, and
turns over the page. He isn't aware that there's any irony in this
remark – how could a three-year-old be!

His mother and I are sitting there, neither of us saying a word.
I'm at a loss for words, the joke is too corny to bother with and his
mother seems to have grown accustomed to ignoring comments of
this sort. So as far as the boy's concerned the father's explanation

goes uncontradicted – by the wives.

11 January 1983 (17 months)
Anneli likes travelling by bus. We're going down the Kudamm* on a number 19. We pass several large posters advertising films, one of them for 'Gone with the Wind'. It shows the profile of a woman's face and part of her body, in a reclining position, her breast partly covered by the neckline of her dress. She is gazing upwards at a large male face bending over her and planting a kiss on her lips.

Anneli says as we drive past, 'Man kissie.' It's the only poster she comments on. Why doesn't she say 'Woman kissie'? Is it because the poster shows the man as the one who's doing something? She's got the message that the man takes the active role. With signals like this we don't need lessons on sex to define gender roles. Is it because we learn these clichés in precisely the same way as we learn to walk, to go to the lavatory, to fasten and unfasten buttons, that it is so hard for us to escape them? This is how things become part of 'nature' and of 'woman's real being'. At this age a child is unable to distinguish between things that are unalterable (like learning to walk, going to the lavatory, doing up buttons) and things that could very easily be changed. She is finding her bearings from things as she sees them.

Anneli's comment corresponds exactly to what is shown on the poster and – with few exceptions – the reality around us.

16 January 1983 (17 months)
Whilst we are shopping in the centre of Berlin we pass a travel agent's with windows full of pictures of bathing beauties in bikinis. Anneli stops, looks at the pictures, and then says 'Woman nothing on.'

18 January 1983 (17 months)
We're waiting at a bus stop next to a newspaper stand. It has the usual display of magazines with cover illustrations of naked and half naked women. Anneli is running around the stall, but then she stops and looks at it. Her comment: 'Woman nothing on.'

We take the bus to the Kudamm. At the corner of Kudamm and

---

* Kurfürstendamm – street in the centre of West Berlin. (*Translators's note.*)

Joachim streets there's a cinema with a huge advertisement outside showing several naked young women in seductive poses. Anneli is looking out of the window as we pass and the poster attracts her attention. Again she says: 'Mummy, woman nothing on.'

1 February 1983 (18 months)
We've been to religious services a few times recently because Anneli has heard music coming from the church and wanted to know what it was. When we see a church she always says the same things: 'Jesale (the baby Jesus), man, children sing, man, lala, man.' To her, 'man' is clearly an integral part of the church and as she always repeats these words in the same order I realise that this is her version of what happens in church. Whenever the children have sung, the man, that is, the vicar, begins to speak. When the organ has been played or when there is some other break in the service the main character, that is, the man, moves to centre stage as the prime motivating force in the action. This is what she means when she repeats the word 'man'.

After our next visit to church she says 'Man talk.'

5 February 1983 (18 months)
In the past few months a friendship has sprung up between Anneli and Schorschi, who is four weeks younger than she is. His mother, Christa, is a friend of mine and the four of us spend a lot of time together.

Of course the two children do not always get on well together. From time to time they have fierce battles – inevitably followed by reconciliation and flinging their arms round one another. In the next few years this friendship with Schorschi is going to be very important in Anneli's development and in my observations I find myself often taking Schorschi as the male figure for comparison.

Whenever Anneli is squabbling with Schorschi, when he prods or pushes her, she screams: 'Ossi not, not hit.' This makes no impression on Schorschi who carries on regardless, with no rebuke from us or reminder that he ought to respect Anneli's wishes. We keep out of it, inclining to the opinion that she has to learn to stick up for herself.

But perhaps this teaches girls that there's no point in having a mind of one's own, if no one takes any notice anyway? Schorschi can ignore it and the adults don't bother. Since the adults don't advocate any norm, then Schorschi's behaviour must be assumed to be okay. These conclusions are obvious to children, boys and girls.

Not until a year later do we encourage a new approach for Anneli to adopt with the slogan: 'If a girl says she doesn't want a thing, then she really doesn't.' And from this time onwards she shows much greater energy in sticking up for herself.

9 February 1983 (18 months)

Anneli and I are with Christa and Schorschi. Schorschi is, as his mother herself says, not as far on in his development as Anneli.

We are playing with the children. I put on a papier mâché mask representing a small bear. This mask is not at all frightening. When Anneli sees it she runs to Christa and cuddles up close to her, burying her head in her arms and peeping out at her disguised mother with only one eye. Schorschi stands opposite me and bends his head towards mine until our foreheads are touching. Then he pulls my hair. When nothing moves he tugs at the mask and after a while succeeds in dislodging it so that I am visible again.

This reminds me of how I once went to a carnival party wearing a Balinese monkey's mask and nobody recognised me. All the girls at the party shuddered at the sight of me, either turning away or shrieking with horror. But the boys tried – some by force – to remove the mask or at least to ascertain the sex of the apparition before them, by grabbing hold of my bottom or breasts.

On the basis of this experience I am at first prepared to interpret Anneli's reaction as typical of a girl and to see in Schorschi a 'real' boy. But I'm puzzled and can't fully understand this behaviour. Is it really innate? And then I remember the children's reactions to St Nicholas and another thought occurs to me. Every teacher knows that children go through phases when they imagine things more vividly and when they are therefore more easily afraid, perceiving dangers to which smaller children are quite oblivious. I hadn't thought of looking at the children's reactions in this light. For Schorschi, whose imaginative powers are not highly developed, the matter was straightforward; he just wanted to remove the thing hiding my head. But Anneli's imagination turned me into a completely different being – she no longer saw me, only the bear. She

Imagination grows at different rates girls first

joined in, but because the game was new to her she took refuge in Christa's familiar arms. Schorschi was unable to play the game because he did not have enough imagination for it.

I wonder how often it happens that children's reactions, due in fact to the stage they have reached in their behavioural development, are interpreted by adults as gender specific? This itself, of course, is bound to influence the child, especially when the interpretation is accompanied by comments of approval from the mother (compare 6 December 1982). Interpretations of this sort, even if they're wrong, increase the stereotyping of the child as girl or boy, and the tendency to treat the child accordingly increases (compare 27 September 1983).[2]

12 February 1983 (18 months)

The TV is switched on for the news. Anneli watches and, after a short time, says 'Man talk.' Then she goes on playing and ignores the television. But after about five minutes she looks at it again. She says 'Man talk.' She's right. And so it continues throughout the whole news programme.

Later on there's a programme about the next general election which I'm keen to see. Although I don't normally watch TV when she's there, I'm too interested in this programme to turn it off. So Anneli watches bits of it. It's a group of men with one woman. Several times Anneli again says 'Man talk.' And when the woman finally manages to get a word in and a female voice is heard Anneli interrupts her game, looks at it with interest and says 'Woman talk.' It's obvious that for her this is not simply a case of people talking one after the other regardless of sex, but that she differentiates precisely between women and men.

14 February 1983 (18 months)

We're walking in the centre of Munich. On an advertising hoarding there's a large advertisement for a film showing a picture of a half naked woman. Once again Anneli annouces 'Woman nothing on.' The fact that she says this so often is beginning to get on my nerves. But she has obviously recognised naked women as a fact of life and feels a need to communicate to me her moments of recognition. I myself have become so blunted to the sight of naked women that I hardly register them any more.

In the evening there is a meeting of a club I'm a member of. I can't find a babysitter and Anneli wants to come with me. Since I'm chairperson I have to go and I take her with me. Inevitably we're fifteen minutes late and a man is just speaking when we arrive. He continues for another five minutes before handing over to me. During this time Anneli whispers to me 'Man talk.' After that I speak for a while and then everyone joins in. On the way home I ask Anneli whether she liked the meeting and all she says is 'Man talk.' I'm simply furious that the man's five minutes of talking have remained the determining factor of the evening for her.

I am depressed by the fact that her perception of how women and men live together can be reduced to one simple formula: 'Woman nothing on – man talk.' She's never said 'Man nothing on', and 'Woman talk' only once.

18 February 1983 (18 months)

We're off tobogganing with Schorschi and his father. Neither of the children is terribly enthusiastic. It's too cold, too uncomfortable, too fast, and I have the impression they're feeling their freedom of movement is restricted – they've scarcely learned and come to terms with walking before they're challenged by another means of locomotion, and an exceptionally rapid one at that. So they are hesitant and careful and don't exactly rush to get on to the sledges – but they don't make any fuss, either. Schorschi's father asks no questions and gives no explanations; he takes a firm hold of Schorschi and sits him on the sledge. Without any hesitation he gives one firm push and they zoom off down the slope. Arriving at the bottom he plonks Schorschi on his tummy on the sledge in order to pull him back up again more easily. Schorschi has difficulty holding on. He's clearly having a struggle, but his father ignores this and simply announces what tremendous fun it all is. The second time Schorschi is put on his tummy for the run down and his father lies on top of him. And it's just as fast as last time. Schorschi has no time to object; on the contrary, his father is firm, even a bit brusque, in his encouragement, simply announcing 'We're great at this, aren't we Schorschi?'

Compare this with my behaviour. We stand for a while at the top looking down at the slope. I explain to Anneli what fun it is and how much other children like tobogganing; then I ask whether

How we speak to the different sex is different *(handwritten margin note)*

she'd like to have a go. And I flatter her, telling her what a big girl she is, and promise to keep tight hold of her. Then we sit on the toboggan and glide down at a comfortable pace.

Afterwards I talk with Schorschi's mother about the difference in our two approaches. She says she has noticed that when she speaks with Anneli she adopts a different tone of voice than when speaking with Schorschi.

We describe our approach to Anneli as affectionate, teasing, mild, gentle, comforting, but with Schorschi we discover that our tone is more challenging and robust, encouraging him to self-reliance, more distant. Who'd have thought it?

24 February 1983 (18 months)

I have noticed recently how often strangers we meet – in the street, in shops and buses – ask Anneli whether she is a girl or a boy. She's only been walking for four months and no child of her age can deal with a question like this. I wonder why it matters, anyway.

Today she announced 'Man drive car.' Was it pure chance that there was a man at the wheel when she noticed this? Or was it because on the whole there are more men driving cars than women? The man almost always takes the wheel and the woman the passenger seat when a couple get into a car. This is the case with Klaus and myself and most of our friends and acquaintances. The man drives; the woman sits next to him and is driven.

No teacher would say to a child, 'Cars are part of the man's world', but they learn it all the same.

11 March 1983 (19 months)

In the afternoon Claudia, aged six, and Anneli play together. Claudia does Anneli's hair. She fastens it up into a knot with a slide and when she brings Anneli into the room Christa and I stand and look at her, telling her how pretty she is and giving her a mirror so that she can admire herself. We don't do anything like this with Schorschi, although he is with us the whole time. Claudia doesn't do his hair and we don't spend any time admiring his appearance.

Once again I notice how gentle Claudia is with Anneli, using her pet name. Her voice has a particularly soft, flattering tone, quite different from that used when addressing Schorschi, with whom she speaks kindly, but in a more neutral and objective voice.

20 March 1983 (19 months)

In the afternoon Anneli and I take the local train to Munich. It's very quiet. A woman of about 45 gets in and sits down opposite us. A conversation develops naturally between her and Anneli, who tells the woman her name. So it's obvious that she's a little girl. The woman tells Anneli that she's on her way home from work, and when Anneli points to her large bag she explains that she intends to do some shopping and then hurry home to tidy up and get the cooking done. Then she adds, 'And when you're a big girl you'll be able to do all that as well.' Anneli nods. I doubt that the woman would have painted a picture of such a future double burden for a little boy.

Preparation of future role of women

4 April 1983 (20 months)

The section on ethnology at the Dahlem museum has exhibits about ships and houses which fascinate children, so I take Anneli.

Like all the other children, she clambers around the ship they're allowed to play on. Inevitably a museum attendant has positioned himself in front of this ship and from time to time he interrupts the children's games to make sure they don't overdo things. In between Anneli approaches the next ship and stretches out her hand to touch the rudder. But she doesn't get that far; the attendant is quicker. His admonishments and prohibitions overawe Anneli and she returns to the play-ship. But from now on, as she investigates the ship, she keeps giving the attendant enquiring glances and her pleasure in the game and her movements are inhibited. Neither of us is enjoying this ship any longer so we go to the South Seas House. This house, although it is open on all sides, can only be entered at one point. When Anneli creeps under the rope we are once again approached by both the attendants present. Now Anneli is feeling really insecure; she takes my hand and whispers, 'Mummy, man tell off.'

9 April 1983 (20 months)

We're at the zoo in Berlin, standing in front of the monkey-house, watching the monkeys chasing one another, picking out fleas and quarrelling. The children love it. Then a large male baboon appears and all the smaller monkeys rush away. I'm almost on the point of saying, in a voice laden with respect, 'Look, here comes the big daddy monkey,' the very tone of my voice enough to show how important this ape is just because he's the father. The same thing happens with the lions. This time I don't manage to choke it back but say without thinking, with special emphasis, 'And that's the daddy lion, look how big he is.' In fact, this daddy lion is walking up and down behind the bars looking just as fed up as all the lionesses, but the tone of my voice and the way I draw attention to him make it clear that *Daddy* really is something special. All the lionesses pale into insignificance by comparison. This is how I pass on patriarchal standards to Anneli. For there's not much point in my selecting emancipated books for her if at the same time I tell her clearly that Daddy is the boss in the family, that he's the greatest, that I as a woman am struck with awe at the very sight of him and that all the other members of the family are subordinate to the biggest – however different daily life in our family may be.

How many other reverent comments of this sort do we women make about males, without noticing it at the time? It's hardly surprising that men have such an incredible advantage over women in commanding respect or that little boys are so self-confident – seeing themselves in the future father role.

15 April 1983 (20 months)
I'm at a Hodler exhibition at the National Gallery in Berlin. Of course, I've brought Anneli with me. In one room where there is a triptych showing two female figures in mannered poses I watch Anneli stand in front of it, trying to imitate the position of the figures. She does this really well, quite catching the manner of the painting.

This reminds me of her behaviour two days earlier when we were looking at fabrics in a department store and she began to imitate the poses of models, assuming amusing contortions. She is quite well able to grasp complex gestures and figures, seeing them as something special and wanting to copy them. But she only ever sees women's figures posed like this: in department stores, at the exhibition, in shop windows and, above all, in advertising hoardings all over the city.

At the exhibition Anneli makes friends with another child and the two of them play together. The attendant devotes all his attention to the two children, never taking his eyes of them. When one of the children finally does touch one of the display cases he rushes over to them and makes a point of admonishing them. Anneli rushes over to me at once. And now the whole authority of the museum is directed at me and I'm accused of all sorts of dereliction of parental duty. I leave without saying a word. To me it was a lot of fuss about nothing. But the man had the final word – he even scolded Mummy!

17 April 1983 (20 months)
We spend quite a lot of time out and about in Berlin and have visited Grunewald and other places popular with day trippers. Everywhere we go there are motor cycles. Anneli is fascinated by them and stops to look at every one, touching them, wanting to sit up on them and occasionally even being allowed to do so. Sometimes, of course, the owners of these machines turn up and stand next to them, donning with great ceremony their leather jackets, crash helmets and all their other gear. Anneli is enormously impressed by all this. And they're always men, every time.

We meet Jürgen in the town at the Café Möhring. And how did he get there? On his motorbike! So her favourite Jürgen has got one – of course, he's a man. And now she has learned to say 'Man – motorbike.' I suppose it was inevitable. But I can't tell her every time we see one that women also ride motorbikes.

Before Anneli is aware of her own sexual identity she knows which areas of life are masculine. She's 20 months old and can say: 'Man talk', 'Man drive car', 'Man motorbike', 'Man kissie', 'Woman nothing on', 'Woman cleaning'.

19 April 1983 (20 months)
I have to buy her some clothes for summer. Anneli's not interested in this at all, since she doesn't care what she wears as long as it doesn't pinch or chafe. So I buy the essentials and we escape from the store. But then when we get home I do want her to try on the things I've bought, to see whether they fit properly. She still doesn't want to and it somehow niggles me now that she shows no interest; after all I've spent money, I'm pleased and I want her to

look nice. I want her to share my pleasure. So when I've put one of the new items of clothing on her I send her into the other room to look in the big mirror and tell her how nice she looks. After doing this a few times Anneli begins to enter into the spirit of the thing and shows pleasure as she stands in front of the mirror. As she does so she looks at me carefully. I know what this glance means: 'I'm a good girl, aren't I, showing such pleasure in my new clothes just to please you.' My attitude has taught her the value of new clothes and of 'being pretty'. She has imitated the emotions I displayed so clearly and they serve as a model, like so many other patterns of behaviour.

I am absolutely sure that if she had been a boy her lack of interest in clothes would not have bothered me in the same way. I wouldn't have expected a boy to share my ideas, but would have accepted his lack of interest, because after all 'he's a boy'. In the case of a daughter it's quite different. A mother cannot tolerate her daughter being different.[3] It's not that I consciously expect her to be just like me, but deep down I can't help measuring my daughter by myself. Divergences are not acceptable; a mother 'saddles her child with her own destiny'.[5]

Simone de Beauvoir even detects this tendency in generous mothers who are trying to do the best for their children. It springs from the conviction that it is better to make a 'true woman' of the child, for society will then more readily accept her.

21 April 1983 (20 months)

We are in the botanic gardens and Anneli is running around not doing any harm to anyone or anything. Three park attendants draw our attention to things we may not do: walk on the grass, step over the chains, shovel up the pebbles on the path. On each occasion it is a man that tells us.

The day before we had been told by one of the male attendants at the zoo that we shouldn't swing on the chains; and a week ago at the market a man told her off for hopping across the corner of material he had laid out for display on the ground. But she has never been told off or forbidden to do anything by women she doesn't know. Is this because people who have the authority to correct children in institutions are always men?

These experiences give Anneli the new magic formula 'Man tell off' to describe all the things she wants to do but suspects are not allowed – like ringing other people's doorbells. She has now reached a stage when she is building up her own sense of authority by giving it a name. That this is happening within a masculine framework is not surprising in view of her experiences over the past few days. In addition she sees that her mother also has to obey the same instructions and prohibitions and occasionally herself makes use of the same magic formula. If only very rarely, I do sometimes employ the 'Man tell off' phrase in order to get out of some difficult situation.

I am slowly beginning to understand why women are more inhibited with men than vice versa; why men have an advantage in exercising authority, especially as superiors; why women are always on the defensive with their boy friends, husbands and male acquaintances; why they always feel they have to do everything right and never make a single mistake. If people in authority are principally men, how can a small girl develop a super-ego?

22 April 1983 (20 months)
In the course of the day Anneli several times asks where all the men we know are: Joachim, Daddy, Hans, Walter. They're all at work, of course, but I myself and other women somehow find time to play with her during the afternoon. The women are either teachers and finish early, or they work part-time, or somehow they make time. Women are more present in her life, but men are surrounded by a mysterious aura of being somewhere else.

Only when this occurs to me now do I realise how often when we are at home in Munich and she asks me where Daddy is do I say 'At work.' And she hears the same thing when she asks where the fathers of her various friends are: 'At work,' the other mothers say. Are the mothers doing nothing at home all day then? Who has brainwashed us, men and women alike, into believing that work is what brings in money and is done away from home? It's partly because mothers, in answer to their children's question as to what Daddy is doing automatically say 'At work', whereas they describe their own activities as cooking, washing, cleaning, clearing up, playing with children, shopping, washing up, etc. – anything but work.

[handwritten note] ✳ No instilling a sense of value on their roles

24 April 1983 (20 months)

Anneli keeps asking me to look at a new picture book she has been given. It tells a cloying story of a little girl and her everyday experiences in a particularly 'feminine' style: 'Today the sun is shining, I must put on my new sun hat, don't I look pretty in it?' She imitates the gestures, putting her finger in her mouth, opening her eyes wide. Of course, there are boys in the book, too, but I call them all children and avoid mentioning their sex. Nevertheless – and I don't know how – whenever a boy appears she immediately gives him the correct sex label. She is obviously already perfectly able to differentiate between the sexes.

In the evening we are at the fountain by the playground. A group of young people of about 20 years old turns up, two young women and two young men with a guitar. The guitarist has long hair and jeans just like the others. For Anneli, though, he is *the man*, and the whole of the evening she keeps talking about him. 'Man play guitar.' I certainly did not refer to him as a man and she did not have enough contact with the group to discover the difference. Is it because he was the main figure in the group? I keep asking myself how she can tell whether a person is a woman, a man, a girl, a boy. Even when there are none of the external signs I thought indicated sex differences to a child she still always gets it right, absolutely correctly and confidently. Perhaps there are signs in expression or movement which a child can recognise but which we no longer notice because our perceptions are too blunted by the obviousness of gender roles.[5]

When we are in foreign countries with languages we do not understand we have to get our bearings by other means. We observe gestures, facial expression, eyes, stance, that is, the whole appearance and so we know who we are dealing with. Why should it be any different for our children? To them, we, the adults, represent the unknown society in which they have to find their way around. With very sensitive perceptions, comparable to fine sensors, they record all details of gender difference which we have grown too blind to see. So just being in society, living in a community, teaches them how to behave correctly as women or men.

26 April 1983 (20 months)
Anneli wants to sit in the driving seat and investigate the car. Of course I let her, but fairly soon, before she herself tires of the game, I put her back into her own child's seat. As we drive off I think about this and I realise I had allowed her less time than Schorschi in the driving seat. Was this because in Anneli's case I was in a hurry? Or did I manage to find more time for Schorschi?

I realise that recently, now her hair has grown longer, I am spending more time doing it, longer than is necessary, really, trying to show her abundant curls to best advantage. I'm convinced that whilst I might have admired a boy's curls, I certainly wouldn't have spent more time dressing his hair.

27 April 1983 (20 months)
We're walking along the street where we live. A couple passes us, a youngish man and a woman of about 40. The woman is carrying a heavy shopping bag. A dialogue about them develops between Anneli and me, the gist of which is as follows:
    Anneli: 'What's the woman carrying?'
    Me: 'A big bag.'
    'What's in it?'
    'Perhaps she's been to the supermarket and now she's taking everything home.'
    'And then she cook.'
    'Yes.'
    'She cook the dinner for her husband.'
    'Perhaps she'll make dinner for her children, not her husband.'
Surprised by her comment, on the spur of the moment I couldn't think of any better explanation.

28 April 1983 (20 months)
I'm at a woman's meeting. One woman gets on to the topic of children and gender differences, stressing how strong they are between her son and daughter, despite the fact she has brought them up the same way. 'It's just the way they are,' she says. She absolutely rejects gender specific education and insists that as a mother she couldn't treat one child differently from the other. But after talking about this for a bit she does remember one difference. 'I do spend longer doing my daughter's hair than my son's; I just

like her to look pretty. I spend as little time as possible doing his. But it's not necessary, he's so good-looking he doesn't need it.'

Ah ha! So that's it! Women and girls have a greater need than men and boys to make themselves beautiful. Man is as he is and can stay that way; he has no need of change or improvement.

1 May 1983 (21 months)

In Berlin we've been visiting several people I know, male and female, and I can't help noticing that the men – with one exception – apart from some bumbling gesture of greeting, don't concern themselves with Anneli at all. They don't address her directly or pay her any other attention. They are friendly but distant and unapproachable, thereby indicating how unimportant she is and how they expect – without saying as much, of course – that she should stay in the background and not disturb them. And she does what's expected of her and never does 'disturb' them.

But their girl friends and wives all do devote some time and attention to Anneli.

2 May 1983 (21 months)

We're driving back from Berlin to Munich. We have a passenger*; at first sight he's like the man in the cigarette ads, and in his attitudes as well, as far as I can tell from our conversation. Anneli keeps trying to make some contact with him. Finally, after several hours, he does address a few words to her, saying with the typically masculine condescension every woman is familiar with, 'Well then, little girl.' She is tremendously impressed by the fact that he has paid her any attention at all, and for several days afterwards she keeps saying 'Man talk – Well then, little girl.' And she gets the tone of voice exactly.

A few things seem to me clear about her contact with men who are not close friends of ours. She has learned that men do not necessarily pay children any of the attention that conventional politeness would normally expect of adults (and here I am not assuming that it would be any different with boys). So a man is apparently permitted to ignore someone; he is in control of the

*Organised by the Car Passenger Agency, a service used quite commonly in Germany which arranges lifts for passengers who share the cost of petrol. (*Translator's note.*)

situation and decides who he will talk to and when. When he does address children, he adopts the tone he will later often use with women. In this way girls are confronted early on with masculine attitudes which will later become very familiar. It's that familiar tone of voice. Later on we no longer notice how condescending and insolent the tone is that men adopt when talking to us, or we only realise afterwards what a cheek it is when a male colleague, who is probably years younger than we are, walks in in the morning and says 'Well, hello girls, how are we this morning?' – though he's little more than a boy himself. But the terms 'girls' and 'boys', in gender relations, have little to do with age. (This, too, the children perceive, as we shall see later.)

3 May 1983 (21 months)
Grandma is visiting us and is playing with Anneli. Some soft toys have been wrapped up and are being rocked to sleep. Grandma shows Anneli how to do it and she copies eagerly.[6] Grandma would never have done this with a boy.

She's brought Anneli a present of a little shopping basket. When we set off to do the shopping in the afternoon I'm on the point of giving it to her and saying 'There, now you've got a shopping basket just like Mummy's', when it occurs to me that by doing so I'm identifying her with me and again defining her in terms of myself and my own activities. Of course, this isn't the first time. How often have I passed on the idea of being 'just like Mummy' in my daily activities as a housewife?

This sense of being just like Mummy, handed on in the daily intimacy between mother and daughter, stays with us all our lives.

4 May 1983 (21 months)
Having been in Berlin for some time Anneli sees Schorschi again for the first time today. Both are delighted. Schorschi gives a whoop of joy when he sees her and runs up to her to embrace her. But sheer exuberance makes the embrace more like a series of thumps. Klaus is watching them and says, admiringly, 'Schorschi's becoming quite a lad.' So Schorschi's clumsiness or physical awkwardness at moments of excitement is interpreted as being real masculine behaviour and is explicitly said to be this in front of the children. No one corrects Schorschi, enlightens or

admonishes him; no one tries to show him what an embrace should be like. His behaviour is simply interpreted as 'masculine'. If it fits what's expected of his sex then there's no need to alter it at all. But men can be so loving!

As soon as Schorschi moves away Anneli goes up to him and is going to try and push him over, in response, no doubt, to his behaviour. But I intervene and tell her not to. I am now expressing my own personal attitude to violent behaviour in children and of course I start with Anneli, not Schorschi.

Perhaps this is pure chance, perhaps not. But Schorschi's behaviour was seen as being typical of a boy and Anneli's stopped and greeted with admonishment instead of acknowledgement.

Christa asks Anneli what she's been doing in Berlin: 'Well, did you have a nice time in Berlin then, Annemariele? Did you go and see the panda bears?' Once again I'm struck by the sweetness and gentleness of her voice and the fact that she uses Anneli's pet name.*

11 May 1983 (21 months)

I take Anneli to the playground. Two mothers are already there, sitting talking whilst their children play in the sandpit: Stefanie, who's a month older than Anneli, and Erich, who's a month younger. These two children know one another very well and often play together, but they don't know Anneli. Anneli wants to use Erich's spade; he doesn't notice, but the girl comes and takes hold of the spade so Anneli can't have it. I interpret Stefanie's action as a form of defence against a stranger who is intruding on the preserve she and her friend have established. The other two mothers see things differently and say as much, loudly: 'The way Stefanie looks after Erich! He doesn't pay any attention at all, but look how she takes care of his things for him. That's just like a man.' (This man is 20 months old.)

Five minutes later, although neither of them know Anneli at all, they comment on Erich being the cheekiest, although he's the youngest. This is because he's been throwing sand around, common enough in both sexes, I would have thought.

*Anneli's full name is Annemarie, but difficulties she had pronouncing this when small led to her being called Anneli. However, it is common in German to add the ending 'le' or 'chen' to people's names when speaking affectionately. (*Translator's note.*)

Later on Erich's mother gives him a bottle of juice which he takes with him and goes on playing. Some time later he drops the bottle and leaves it on the path; he doesn't need it any longer, but doesn't bring it back to his mother. Soon Anneli says to me, in the same voice she uses to comment on all the events of life, 'Erich lost bottle' (just like 'Dustmen noisy'), and brings me the bottle. The two other mothers are simply ecstatic at the way in which Erich's bottle is being taken care of and are impressed because Anneli, too, is looking after Erich. They go on at some length in front of the children about how touching it is to see such little girls worrying about the 'men'.

A few days later I hear the same thing from a friend of mine. She keeps noticing that a four-year-old friend of her son's, a girl, knows more about his clothes than he does and even puts his shoes on for him; at playgroup this little girl is always looking after little boys of the same age. A playgroup supervisor who lives near us confirms how considerate little girls are.

I wonder in fact how much it is that some skill or dexterity girls chance to show is picked up, reinterpreted and then taken advantage of to get things done more quickly, both at home and at playgroup, until it's just taken for granted.

14 May 1983 (21 months)

Some time ago we noticed that the three-year-old daughter of an artist friend of ours was wearing a ring her father had made for her. We liked it very much and asked him if he'd make one for Anneli. Today he brought her it and said: 'At first, children can't get used to wearing rings, you just have to keep trying.' Anneli was delighted with this present, but the artist was absolutely right about the problems of wearing it. We told her that everybody wore a ring and she showed it to everyone proudly. But then she'd had enough. I gave up trying to persuade her and put the ring aside for later.

I'm convinced that neither our friend nor we would have spent any time at all encouraging a boy to wear a ring, assuming we'd bought him one in the first place.

I have noticed that Anneli is becoming rather aggressive towards Schorschi, shoving him and even hitting him occasionally – and he her. I tell her not to do this and have once or twice really scolded her for it. I have an absolute aversion to physical violence and cannot bring myself to ignore her behaviour just because she's supposed to respond in kind to boys. But it's always me who tells Anneli to stop shoving and thumping whilst Schorschi's mother rarely puts him right.

15 May 1983 (21 months)

Anneli and I went to see some friends this afternoon and the visit has stuck in my mind. I wonder whether this is because of the behaviour of our hostess's eleven-year-old son, and decide it must be. He spent so much time playing very affectionately with Anneli, and that made it unlike other visits we have paid to families with boys. Normally, older boys don't spend any time at all with her; they just ignore her as though she weren't there. Thus they display their masculine disregard for women (compare 1 May 1983). That's quite normal, and I've become so used to such behaviour that I was almost put out by the caring approach of this boy and could hardly believe it.

18 May 1983 (21 months)

I have been busy sewing cute little buttons on her jeans, blouses and dresses; they are brightly coloured and depict little animals, fruit, etc. And I can't help but enjoy seeing the sweet little girl in Anneli and wanting to cuddle her. I want her to look nice when we have visitors or when we do something special. In general, I notice I tend to buy bright, cheerful colours for her, often choosing pink, red, turquoise, yellow or light blue. Ellen, on the other hand, says that for her four-year-old son she tends to choose blue, brown, maroon, grey, green, etc. and won't buy anything too fashionable – it has after all got to be suitable for a boy.

22 May 1983 (21 months)

We're in Italy with Christa and Schorschi. It's warm and Schorschi is wearing a pair of shorts and Anneli jeans. Then she pulls the elastic round the bottom up to her knees and now she's wearing shorts, too. So Christa and I decide she's developing an eye for clothes and that dress is becoming important to her, and that it's all because she's a girl. We just go wittering on, seeing something feminine in the quite simple act of imitation. Really she probably just wants to be dressed the same as the other child and copied Schorschi because it was hot and the jeans were uncomfortable. Schorschi, on the other hand, was feeling okay and had no reason to change. He'd probably do the same thing in her place, but we wouldn't interpret that as being typically feminine.

We can't seem to get away from thinking in these stereotypes.

30 May 1983 (21 months)

On the beach Anneli hasn't got any knickers on, but is just wearing a short smock that covers her bottom and has two slits at the side. It's horizontally striped in bright colours. Two boys' mothers are sitting on the beach admiring the smock and saying what a pity it is they can't dress their little sons (who are the same age) in anything as pretty as that. And later on I hear exactly the same thing from another boy's mother.

I can't for the life of me understand why a twenty-one-month-old boy can't wear a smock – after all, our grandparents' generation all wore smocks until they were three years' old.

A few days later I see a picture of Bismarck as a child with his brothers and sisters. Try as I will I cannot recognise Bismarck from his clothes. All the children are wearing either smocks or dresses. So where is the lad? But in spite of this no one doubted Bismarck's manliness in later life.

1 June 1983 (22 months)

During the holiday we've just been having with Schorschi and Christa, as well as playing together happily and unproblematically, the children have developed one particular set pattern of behaviour. At the start, both children are playing happily on their own, then Schorschi stops what he's doing and goes over to Anneli, then there are some variations.

1. Schorschi gives Anneli a shove so that she falls over and starts to yell.
2. He aims a few blows at her with his hand or some object he's picked up; she starts yelling but he carries on doing this.
3. He pushes her over and then hits her; she starts yelling.
4. He takes whatever it is she's playing with away from her; if

she holds it tight he takes it by force. Anneli starts yelling, turns away and comes to me, or else she finds something else to play with. Schorschi now puts the toy he has taken from her down somewhere; it no longer interests him. If Anneli goes on playing, the whole game starts from the beginning again.

5. Schorschi goes up to Anneli with some threatening gesture, shouting 'ggrrh' or something similar and pushes Anneli back into the corner of the room. Her shout of 'no' has no effect on him at all.

Only rarely does Schorschi's mother tell him to stop, and he's not the only one who behaves like this. It's not because he's an aggressive little monster; he's a thoroughly normal, likeable little lad; he speaks less fluently than Anneli, but is more independent in his play.

I have noticed this type of behaviour in all the other little boys on the beach, both German and Italian. Shoving and taking other children's toys away from them seem to play a special part in the social life of small male children. The fact that Anneli does not hit him back surprises me at first, until I leaf through my diary and see how often I have told her not to. Oddly enough once again the things I have observed fit perfectly with theory.[7]

Anneli's yelling and her constant search for new toys gets on my nerves, as do her constant evasions. And it annoys me that no one ever tells the boys to stop behaving as they do. So I discuss with Christa and the other boys' mothers what is apparently only a problem for me as the mother of a girl. I ask them why they never intervene. Without exception all the boys' mothers put forward the same theory. That is, that when children are bickering adults shouldn't intervene; the children have to work out their own little squabbles for themselves (they are 21 months old). And they say it's particularly important for girls to learn to stand up for themselves against boys. Franziska says, 'Do you want your daughter to grow up vulnerable and defenceless, a regular little hothouse plant? You of all people should think it's important that later, at playgroup and school, she can stick up for herself with the boys, that she doesn't just have to put up with everything but can compete on equal terms. She has to start early, Marianne. The girl must learn to defend herself, be self-reliant in a struggle instead of giving up or running to Mummy. After all, in later life girls will have to come to terms with men and look after themselves.'

It's all true, but even so I don't like it. In reality it means that Anneli has to learn to be as aggressive as her fellows. Claudia, Schorschi's elder sister, said to her once: 'Hit him back.' So she did. Whereupon a thoroughly nasty little scene developed, with two little children having a go at one another. In the end Anneli came to me shouting, 'Schorschi keep hitting.' She could see how stupid it all was.

In my opinion the theory of the boys' mothers that the children have to regulate their own interactions and girls learn to defend themselves is just one more lie to cheat girls. Since adults do not show their disapproval of force or of taking things from others, patterns of behaviour are determined by male children and girls have to fit in with them, whether or not it suits their mood at the time. Girls have to learn to adapt, because for the rest of their lives they're going to have to fit in with what men want. This seems to me to be a modern variation on an age-old theme.

It's quite different for a boy. He is accepted, aggressive as he is. 'It's just that boys hit out more readily' is a phrase you hear all the time. It may even be that the boys' mother herself goes to classes on methods of non-violent defence and is active in the peace movement, whilst at the same time she lets her son have his way when he releases his petty aggressions on other children in a sandpit.

Regardless of how the girl learns to deal with aggressive situations, one thing she does grasp is that *she* has to learn something, something determined by boys. She has to act like a boy. They must be doing the right thing because they are allowed to stay the way they are. The children are not told that force can never be a means of settling a disagreement, certainly not if girls don't like it. Why doesn't it occur to the boys' mothers that their sons are going to have to get along with women later, and girls fairly soon at play-group and school, and that both girls and women do not like violence, hitting and shoving? Why doesn't anyone say to little boys 'Stop it, girls don't like it', instead of 'Stand up for yourself against that boy'? When I suggested this all I got as an answer was: 'But he's going to have all sorts or problems in the future if he starts measuring himself against girls now.'

Of course, what a blight that might be on his masculinity!

2 June 1983 (22 months)
In Italy it's warm enough for the children to run around without any clothes. When they pee, Schorschi does the same as Anneli, crouching next to her.

When Christa is taking a shower Anneli joins her and after watching her for a time says 'Christa girl.' I have never explained to her that girls grow into women or that women were once girls, so I'm surprised at how early the connection between woman and girl is clear. Now, of course, she's able to notice the similarities in the behaviour of women and girls and to see how they are different from the other group of human beings.

3 June 1983 (22 months)
We go out to buy a pair of summer shoes. In the shop the assistant brings me four likely pairs. I reject patent leather and black shoes. Of the two remaining pairs I select the ones with decorative stitching that are rather fashionable. The other pair are quite plain with just a simple leather strap over the instep. Only afterwards does it occur to me that I have chosen the pair that are quite unmistakably girls' shoes. I function like a machine, reacting as expected to the traditional categories: I accept the obvious, as intended. The correct shoes for a girl to wear are the ones that indicate at once that she is a girl.

14 June 1983 (22 months)
Mothers sit talking while the children play in the play area.

Four-year-old Hanna is playing on the apparatus with great enthusiasm. She climbs higher and higher, moving with absolute confidence and in no apparent danger. Then her mother rushes across to her, drags her from the climbing frame, enfolds her in loving, protective arms and says: 'Darling, you could fall off there, it's dangerous to climb so high.' Daughter yells but mother finds an alternative diversion for her in the sand playing with little Anneli. Peace is restored.

We continue our conversation and Hanna's mother now tells me of her five-year-old son's hobbies. 'He loves making things, and sometimes it is dangerous when he's using tools or a knife, but a boy's got to learn to judge this for himself. It's no good just taking the things from him or forbidding him to use them. There is a risk involved, but that's part of being a boy; otherwise he doesn't feel right.'

17 June 1983 (22 months)

We are visiting a friend with a four-year-old son. The boy is fiddling around the balcony door, and an argument and some confusion ensue because he can't close it the way he wants to. Then his mother says in front of both of the children: 'Boys are awful, always up to something. But what can you do about it? Girls are different; they naturally behave more quietly and more sensibly.'

Of course, girls mess around with doors and do silly things, too – but it's not automatically put down to their sex, the way it is with boys; they're just told to stop it.

Two hours later Anneli also has a go at the door, inspired no doubt by the boy's example. Then our hostess goes across to her, takes her arm, saying, 'Come away from there, Anneli, you might hurt yourself,' and leaves the room, holding Anneli protectively in her arms.

18 June 1983 (22 months)

We have been invited to a birthday party in the country. There are lots of parents there with their children, most of them about the same age as Anneli, including Thomas, who is six months older, with his father. It being a Bavarian party there is a barrel of beer to be tapped.* Thomas is sitting on his father's lap watching this exciting event. His father tells him, 'Now, Thomas, pay attention and watch what they do. If you ever hope to be Lord Mayor of Munich watch carefully how they tap a barrel of beer properly.'

Leaving aside the humour of this exhortation I suddenly realise that it would never occur to me to think that Anneli might become Lord Mayor of Munich – not even as a joke. Such a future for her is absolutely inconceivable to me.

So now I've got to the point where, though I might lay claim to positions of seniority for myself, I'm discounting them for my daughter. Have I forgotten that I wanted the world to be her oyster?

19 June 1983 (22 months)

I've just had a shower and am standing in the bath. I haven't heard

---

*The reference here is to the ceremonial tapping of the first barrel of beer by the Lord Mayor at the *Oktoberfest*, the famous Munich beer festival. (*Translator's note.*)

Anneli coming up behind me, but suddenly she smacks me on the bottom, shouting 'Pitsh, patsh.' She's taken me by surprise and I tell her to stop, but she hops around with delight, laughing. Though I don't scold her I do tell her I don't think it's nice to hit people.

A short time afterwards a nursery school teacher I happen to meet tells me that boys all like scrapping so much because their fathers play so many rough and tumble games with them at home.

So I begin to think about this. Klaus and I keep Anneli from any form of physical attack by the way we react to any gestures of this sort she may make. Is this really because we're so opposed to violence, or because deep down it doesn't fit our idea of Anneli because she's a girl?

When I've seen fathers rolling on the floor in some mock battle with their sons I've never been shocked or thought of their game as a form of physical violence. Only now do I realise how often I have seen scenes such as this among friends who have small sons. I have taken these games completely for granted without it ever occurring to me that this is yet another form of gender education. For this reason I now have to assume that the opposite is true – that I automatically discourage violence in Anneli because she's a girl.

A few hours later, when she's playing with clay at a neighbour's house, I have the opportunity to see what physical strength she has and how she enjoys employing it. She's banging a soft piece of clay with enormous energy, strength and stamina. As I watch her I suddenly think that this is a side of her I don't know.

Later in the afternoon we've been invited out and I fasten up her curls with a slide she has been given recently. With her hair done like this, she suddenly looks so pretty, so fragile and in need of protection. She's my sweet little daughter and I can't help putting my arms round her, though she herself is just on the point of dashing off. To delay her for a moment I admire her, telling her how beautiful I think she is. Of course, it's all the same to her and I'm aware that she stays with me in order to please me. Her expression is a reflection of my pleasure in her. Another reminder of girls' 'innate' tendency to vanity and dressing up.

26 June 1983 (22 months)
Whilst Anneli is running around in Grandma's garden without any

clothes on she puts her finger into her vagina. This seems quite normal to me, not a form of excessive sexual gratification, but simply pleasure in feeling her own body – she might just as well have stuck her finger up her nose. Grandma turns to me and says, 'I think there's something wrong with her there again. An inflammation or infection [she did have one when she was a baby], because she's always touching herself there.' And Grandma goes up to Anneli and says, 'You'll hurt yourself if you do that. You shouldn't touch yourself there,' and then follows this with a highly suggestive question, 'It hurts there, doesn't it?' Anneli looks at Grandma with surprise. Is what was pleasurable for her now being turned into pain? Is suffering now being connected with that part of her body, whereas with a boy it would be said that he'd discovered his penis and was now enjoying playing with it, since it's such a good toy. This is all so serious for women – either it doesn't exist or it hurts!

29 June 1983 (22 months)
In the afternoon some people we know are having a party to which a lot of children have been invited.

Our hostess is standing on the stairs outside and tells us how much her two boys (one-and-three-quarters and two-and-three-quarter years old) like climbing up the railings. For the sake of saying something I note that they must need good muscles for it and then casually tell Anneli to show the muscles in her arm; I flex my biceps as an example. Claudia (7 years old) and Christa are there, too. So as a joke I tell them to show us their muscles and let Claudia feel my flexed biceps. She imitates me. But her mother gives a slightly embarrassed smile, giggles a bit and says, 'I haven't got any muscles, you've no need to feel them, there's nothing there,' and she lets her arms hang down by her sides. Claudia is disappointed and looks thoughtfully from one to the other of us. Anneli listens to all this with interest. Of course Christa has muscles, well developed muscles, from lugging her two-year-old son around in her arms whenever he asks, from doing the garden and the housework. But once again it's only men's muscles that count; muscles means men. A woman simply doesn't have any. She's all skin and fat, I suppose?

30 June 1983 (22 months)

We go out for a walk to a small lake. A group of school children is there. Anneli goes across to the children, who are about 12 years old, and in no time at all is surrounded by girls who play with her, one of whom finally brings her back to us. Once again, not one of the boys has taken any notice of her at all or exchanged a single word with her. Men are in a world apart and by ignoring her they show her that they are different.

In the evening I happen to read an article which says that fathers always do what children find interesting, whereas mothers are stuck with the housework which is monotonous.[8] I can only agree with this. During the day any mother who does not have servants spends most of her time occupied with housework. And that really is monotonous: tidying up, shopping, cooking, washing, ironing, cleaning, etc. In the evenings, however, when Daddy comes home, things look up, for at last someone's arrived who is able to spend time with the children without being continually interrupted by menial household tasks, who can devote himself to them and think up new games. But mother's in the kitchen – what a bore. For her part, of course, mother is glad to have a bit of time to herself at last, time to think without the constant questions of the children, knowing that someone is taking care of them. Since the family has to eat, the cooking has to be done – and mother connects being on her own with cooking. I'm always relieved to be able to escape to the kitchen and hand Anneli over to her father after being with her continually from seven in the morning. Most of the interesting things mothers might do with their children get swallowed up in the daily routine of housework; the rest are few and far between.

4 July 1983 (23 months)

Grandma helps Anneli to make a garage of building bricks for her numerous toy cars. She asks, 'Where on earth did you get them all from? You're a girl!'

We visit friends in the afternoon. Another woman with a son the same age as Anneli is also there. Right at the start they unpack all the toys they have brought with them. And what are they? Nothing but cars. We haven't brought anything with us because I think Anneli ought to explore the things around her. Grandma's comment of this morning, that is, that of a conservative 65-year-old, is borne out by the actions of this boy's mother, who is a 30-year-old social worker and educationalist, and no doubt believes she is progressive. What Anneli sees coincides with what her grandma had said; it all fits, and one thing gives added weight to another.

So why didn't I take any cars along for her to play with? Because of my aversion to turning what is an object of daily use into a fetishistic toy that children play with all the time. In this at least I am able to succeed with my daughter. I don't know whether I'd make any concessions if she were a boy.

5 July 1983 (23 months)

We're staying in the Engadine, in Switzerland, once again and once again four-year-old Martin and his mother, Ellen, are with us. He has grown particularly fond of fighting recently and tries to start up a scrap at every opportunity. His mother just wards him off. But I join in and when we are having a rest during a ramble he runs at me head down. He is the weaker, of course, and absolutely helpless in my grasp. Just like when he's doing this with his father. Then his mother addresses me reproachfully: 'Why are you so hard on the poor lad? You don't have to make him the loser straight away.'

It's all right if his father proves to be the stronger in a struggle. Only in the case of a woman is violence recognised for what it is and called by name. But even then, a woman is supposed not to show the comparative strengths as they really are – even in fun. Even towards such a little man a woman has to be the weaker.

But Martin has learned something new and so has Anneli, for she watched it all with interest.

10 July 1983 (23 months)

Now we're on holiday Klaus and Anneli spend a lot of time together and they really enjoy this. Klaus acknowledges that his behaviour towards his daughter is particularly affectionate and that he can't imagine that he would speak to her with quite so much flattery, sympathy and persuasiveness if she were a boy. He notices that he is much more brisk and more succinct with Schorschi. But he also thinks he tends to let Schorschi get on with things, whereas he will bring Anneli across to where he himself is and cajole her into joining him.

He's convinced he wouldn't want to touch and hold a boy so much. It would be embarrassing with a boy, he says; he cannot imagine so much physical contact with another man, however small that man might be. He thinks that for him there is always an erotic element in a cuddle and that cuddling is therefore only possible with a girl.

16 July 1983 (23 months)

Once again I can't help noticing how much Ellen changes her intonation and vocabulary when she is talking with Anneli rather than Martin. With Anneli she often talks baby language and the pitch is much higher; her voice is altogether more gentle. Is it possible that the only reason for this is the difference in the children's ages?

We've been doing a lot of walking. We pass lots of streams and pools and every time we come to some patch of water, even when Martin himself doesn't notice it, his mother says to him, 'There's a smashing stream, you can do a nice pee into that,' or 'Look, don't you want to piddle into that pond?' Every time, he meets this summons in grandiose fashion and the penis is produced to exclamations of maternal praise. Both of them find an obvious delight in the ceremony which far exceeds the relief natural to emptying the bladder. It is a delight in demonstrating his sex as a tool, as something that goes beyond the individual.

That this tool is used from the very earliest age to create a sense of solidarity among men, the triumph of 'We men'[9] as against the oft bemoaned lack of solidarity among women, is demonstrated even more clearly two days later when Martin's father joins us.

After grilling sausages over an open fire the father summons his son: 'And now we men will put the fire out.' And then the two of them stand side by side, legs apart, and urinate into the hissing, smoking embers. The only role in this for the women present seems to be that of wondering admirers. If I put myself in the place of two-year-old Anneli, who watches it all with the natural curiosity she has for the world around her, then penis envy seems inevitable.

She sees that there are two categories of human being. The one group are called men and boys and they have toys dangling between their legs which earn them praise and admiration, such admiration being offered them by the second category, that is, the girls and women, who are not in possession of such admirable devices with which to command attention. The conclusion the child must draw is obvious, for she never sees women playing games of this sort.

Every child wants to have the others' interesting toys, but not every refusal of a toy leads to the same lifelong inferiority complex attributed to women on account of their 'penis envy'. The 'toy', then, clearly has some additional meaning. It is not only the sight of the penis that is able, as Helen Deutsch stresses, to influence the inner development of the girl: 'the sight of the boy's penis is not the sole traumatic event that changes her life; it is the last link in a long chain.'[10] Life makes it quite clear why girls feel this inner lack.

Simone de Beauvoir writes: 'pride in his manhood is instilled into him; this abstract notion takes on for him a concrete aspect: it is incarnated in his penis. He does not spontaneously experience a sense of pride in his sex, but rather through the attitude of the group around him.'[11]

After this holiday the words 'woman' and 'man' play an active part in Anneli's vocabulary, are used often and are contrasted with one another.

18 July 1983 (23 months)
In the car Ellen is joking with the children. She asks Anneli 'Are you a girl or a boy?' This question doesn't mean anything to Anneli in relation to herself, because so far – at least consciously – I have only referred to her as a child. I have often been on the point of talking about girls and boys but I always stopped myself because I felt that by doing so I would divide Anneli's world too soon into two separate parts. And each time I noticed that when I was going to use the words 'girl' or 'boy' I was differentiating, albeit according to very diffuse principles not clear to myself. I felt at such moments that this polarisation was limiting, a minus in comparison to 'person' or 'child'. With either of these I am leaving everything open – Anneli still has the *whole* palette of life experiences ahead of her; if I left the sex open I could, and she should, think, imagine and envisage that her future contained everything the world and life have to offer a human being and not

just that paltry segment intended for a woman. I wanted to keep this illusion for Anneli as long as possible and not force her to early self-definition. I wanted to keep her from the selective perception of what a girl or boy does or is allowed to do and hoped she would be able to grow in accordance with her own wishes and temperament for as long as possible. That she was already able to divide the rest of the world into men and women was, of course, perfectly clear to me.

19 July 1983 (23 months)

The day before Martin's father joined us on holiday everything that was in any way out of the ordinary was put off until later with the comment, 'Daddy will do that with you.' This includes going on the chairlift, making a fire, a long mountain trip. And all these adventures really do happen once Daddy's arrived. Martin's even allowed to go scrambling up the rockier slopes.

In the evening, when the children have been put to bed, Ellen, as the more experienced mother (her son is after all two years older), explains now, from the age of about four, children develop an absolute admiration for their father. She wonders what causes this but thinks it probably has something to do with the Oedipus complex. After what I've heard it doesn't surprise me at all.

Many of the things that the father did during the day aroused admiration, such as throwing a stone a really long way or jumping down from a crag. Every time, Ellen draws her son's attention to this with words like 'Look how far Daddy can jump . . . or throw . . . or . . . '

And all the time I've been there not a single word has been uttered about how marvellous the diverse achievements of us women are. Not surprising, then, that the son sees his father as omniscient and omnipotent in contrast to his mother. It's possible to do so many more marvellous things with him.

'In the eyes of the child the father embodies . . . strength, the ideal, the outside world,' said Winnicott generations ago.[12] The mother is stuck in her daily routine, she embodies house and household. And women encourage this fantasy!

25 July 1983 (23 months)

After the time spent with Martin and his father, Anneli has

completely changed her manner of passing water. She refuses to crouch down to pee and if she can't stand out of doors she clambers on to the lavatory seat and, standing or kneeling, directs a stream into the bowl. She's very good at it. Martin, on the other hand, pees, as his mother says, hexagonally, and afterwards the lavatory seat has to be cleaned. But nobody has ever suggested he sit down.

It's obvious to me why Anneli does this, after all we've heard. And in the meantime there have been more conversations between father and son which were bound to influence Anneli.

Whenever Martin has managed a little crap in the loo, it's praised as being just like a man's; if Martin has hurt himself and bleeds a little, it's described as being real man's blood; at mealtimes he's told to eat his food like a man, just like Daddy.

But no one has ever thought of telling Anneli that her pee was real female urine or that she should eat up her food like a real woman. Being a woman has never been put to her in this way, as something to aspire to. Ellen and I haven't been presented as models worthy of emulation, either by ourselves or anyone else.

The origins of penis envy are no longer a mystery to me.

26 July 1983 (23 months)
We're at the playground and Anneli is playing in the sand. Two children arrive, a boy and a girl, about six and five years old. As they play the boy continually orders the girl about. She obeys and 'helps' him when he tells her to. Then he gives the order to go, puts on his socks and shoes and moves about five metres away. She is left behind, an absolute picture of misery sitting on the ground and whingeing at him to wait for her. With a magnanimous gesture he turns round and says curtly, 'Hurry up, then.' The girl fumbles nervously with her socks and shoes and then runs after him like a little dog.

All the time these children were there Anneli was standing next to me watching them. She didn't say or do anything, but was clearly affected by what she saw. As the children were leaving she then referred to the boy as such. She can recognise his sex, and she can tell the girl from her clothes.

As we stand there and watch I can't help wondering what impression this is making on her. I'm inclined to believe that children absorb events around them uncritically in order to imitate them later and it makes me shudder to think that this could provide a model for behaviour. But what happened does concur with other observations she has already made. It all seems to fit and for girls masculine dominance does appear to be one of the facts of life.

27 July 1983 (23 months)

Grandma tells me to buy Anneli a summer dress and obediently we repair to a shop that sells children's clothes. She has to try things on. When she starts complaining and doesn't want to have anything to do with it all (it's her first dress) the assistant tells her the usual story of how pretty she is and that she should look at herself in the mirror. I don't really care whether we buy the dress or not so I don't join in this game of persuasion, but the shop assistant does succeed in dragging her to the mirror and stopping the crying at least temporarily. Anneli has once again fallen for the 'Aren't you pretty!' trick. So we buy the dress and go home. Inevitably I now want to show her father what a 'lovely' dress we've bought and Anneli has to try it on again. Of course, she doesn't want to and starts bawling again; she's completely indifferent to the dress. So now we both join in – after all, this pretty little article has cost us £20 and we want to see something for our money. We finally manage to persuade her by telling her that one of our neighbours, whom she knows and very much likes, will admire her dress and her appearance and that she must show her it. So Anneli puts the dress on, runs round to the neighbour's and is accordingly admired. Now she's really enjoying herself, for she likes admiration.

If this isn't the way to teach your daughter vanity and typically female behaviour, to show her how to please people, to make herself pretty to gain admiration, then I don't know what is. Feminine vanity is hardly innate.

28 July 1983 (23 months)

I often encourage Anneli to talk to people. Today at the station I suggested that she go up to a child who was crying to see what the matter was and to comfort her. And she did.

In the evening one of our neighbours is giving a birthday party. We've been invited and since I know it's a 75th party and important I persuade Anneli to put on her new dress and a coral necklace.

She looks really pretty and is much admired. A repetition of yesterday's situation: practice makes perfect.

29 July 1983 (23 months)

Anneli comes home from her babysitter's with bright pink make-up on her cheeks. She wanted to paint herself just like Tini, and so Tini made her up. 'If it had been a boy I wouldn't have done it, of course, because a boy is after all a boy,' is Tini's reply to a question from me.

I have given Anneli a little work bench for hammering on, just like one I had seen in a room belonging to two boys. Hammering in nails is a practical thing to learn and she soon gets the hang of it.

Again we see, a girl may take to tools, but not a boy to make-up. For her it's an advantage to be able to use tools like a boy. But it's absolutely ridiculous for a boy to learn to use make-up; it might make him gay, a nightmare thought at the back of many boys' mothers' minds.

We go to Ellen's. Anneli hops and jumps around the place with great glee. Then Ellen picks her up in the middle of her dance and asks her suggestively whether she'd like to be a ballet dancer in a pink skirt. Anneli says 'yes' and looks at Ellen seriously and thoughtfully. She clearly finds what Ellen has said quite interesting. If a girl starts hopping and dancing for sheer joy conclusions are drawn, as though movement weren't something normal but has to be interpreted as being somehow out of the way.

4 August 1983 (2 years)

Back again to the theory of penis envy. Anneli is one of a small group of children at a playgroup. When they all decide to have a pee Max stands up to do it, holding a basin under his penis. Anneli stands and watches him, as she watches other children, and then she says, 'Max willie.'

Afterwards the children play at trains. For whatever reason, perhaps because he's a year older, Max decides he's going to be the train driver and he orders the others – three girls – around. Same again with a shopping game: he is the self-appointed boss and does the selling; the girls have to do as they're told and buy what he wants.

It seems inevitable that Anneli and the other girls will see a connection between his anatomy and everything he's allowed to do. The playgroup organiser allows him to take the lead continually; she even joins in herself and lets him boss her around.

17 August 1983 (2 years)
We are visiting a family with two daughers (four and seven years old). The three children tear around, first in the garden and then outdoors when we go for a walk, letting off steam to their heart's content. The parents watch them from the coffee table and explain, 'They're real tomboys – but we don't mind.' Thus they show how progressive and liberal they are so far as education is concerned. This statement seems to me to be important for two reasons. First, it shows that there are two completely different starting points when considering the motor functions of boys and girls and that in everything they do children are classified as being typical or untypical of their sex. Human behaviour, with varying natural talents and preferences, does not exist. Secondly, girls are not only expected to behave in the way prescribed for them, but may *also* behave like boys; if their parents are *really* progressive (and I sometimes think I'm one of them) then they will be *expected* to do so.

But it's dreadful that behaviour which is not gender typical so depends on parental approval ' . . . but we don't mind'. The giving of permission in itself includes the constraint that it may at any time – and as far as the children are concerned there is neither rhyme nor reason in this – be revoked by the adults. How far a girl may diverge from accepted gender behaviour patterns depends entirely on their good will and passing mood.

However liberal their parents may be, girls notice the limits of such freedom when the parents are under stress, when the mother or father is not able to think calmly and clearly about traditional expectations. At nine o'clock in the evening, after a tiring day, parents are more likely to expect peace and quiet from their noisy, energetic daughters than sons, or are more likely to demand it, for it's all to easy then to say: 'Why are they behaving like boys?'[13]

So the girl becomes aware that 'behaving like a boy' – without even considering the effect of any particular stress in the words – is the exception; that she's really not intended to tear around or indulge in rough and tumble games.

19 August 1983 (2 years)

Today is Anneli's birthday. Klaus decides to give her some flowers and at the florist's he asks for a bouquet suitable for a small child. The florist asks 'Is it a boy or a girl?' In response to Klaus's answer the saleswoman then says she can use any colours and makes up a bright mixture of pink and violet! Maybe she's a feminist.

I wonder what colours would have been thought suitable for a boy and why?

20 August 1983 (2 years)

It's been a long, hot summer. Anneli likes running around without any clothes on both indoors and in the garden. But whenever we slip out to the supermarket we have problems if Klaus is at home. He insists that she puts something on, even if it's only a T-shirt and a pair of knickers. I don't think it's worth arguing about. I'd let her run around without anything on – even in the supermarket or in the street.

Klaus and I discuss this. He doesn't like his daughter being seen naked in the street, but he can't explain why. When he thinks about this more carefully he only says that he feels uneasy and doesn't want any number of other people seeing his daughter without any clothes on.

A woman friend who's a social worker visits us and we talk about this subject with her as well. I also explain how I sometimes let Anneli wear a smock that only reaches to her bottom, without any knickers. Then she can have a pee whenever she likes, standing up or crouching down, without needing any help.

Boys' mothers had given me the idea for this by saying that they felt sorry for girls because they have to crouch down to relieve themselves or be told they have to wait, and by generally expressing themselves very disparagingly about girls.

My friend shakes her head thoughtfully and says she wouldn't let Anneli run around naked because of child molesters. We decide that considerations of this sort do not affect us directly – since at the moment I am always with Anneli – but do have general relevance. Anneli's naked innocent body could motivate a man to seek a victim elsewhere. I don't want the sight of Anneli to put other children at risk, so I decide not to allow her to run about without her clothes on or at least not without her knickers on.

I draw three conclusions from this. First, the way girls pee is made a subject of ridicule and a girl disparaged because of her anatomy; in addition, female clothing is such that other ways of relieving oneself are impossible, given the realities of present-day society. Secondly, according to relevant theoretical works, fathers are more conservative as far as gender specific upbringing is concerned.[14] I thought that might be true of other fathers, but not of Klaus. But even he reacts in accordance with the statistics. Isn't he, in his own cultural sphere, behaving just like a Moslem who cannot tolerate his wife going out without a veil? Thirdly, I am putting the feeling of freedom and pleasure in one's own body second to the consideration of what effect this might have on masculine behaviour, whether Anneli herself or other females might come to harm. Even though this last consideration may include only a tiny percentage of all men, nevertheless the figure is clearly high enough to have a controlling effect on women's behaviour. At the same time I realise this is a tacit agreement with the masculine argument on rape: 'If she hadn't behaved like that or been dressed like that then he would never have assumed . . . ' Once again a girl adapts to the masculine world without even noticing why. We wouldn't call that education – or would we? I'm denying Anneli delight in her beautiful body because of some foul characters and I'm furious.

21 August 1983 (2 years)

We are in Berlin. Anneli is wearing a light summer dress. When we've left the house Klaus realises she hasn't got any knickers on – one of us has forgotten to put them on her. I think, 'So what? I sometimes go without myself in the summer.' Klaus, however, is horrified and would like to turn back to get her some knickers. When I ask him why he says that without her knickers she won't be able to sit down wherever she likes! I can't see this and reckon that on a hot dry day like today she can sit down anywhere. Why not? 'Because she might get some dirt there.' Where, for goodness sake?

Two hours later we are in Grandma Rosner's garden. She has made a sand box for Anneli and I put her into it – naked. As soon as Grandma Rosner sees that she runs in to get some pants for Anneli and is determined to put them on, despite Anneli's energetic resistance. She's says she's doing this because if Anneli sits naked in the sand she might get 'something between her legs'. The child will be bathed anyway, between her legs as well, so what is it that makes girls so vulnerable there?

Only now does it occur to me that Grandma in Munich also spends all summer running after Anneli to put some knickers on her – that at the very least! Her reason was that 'without' she can't sit down everywhere. Once again this dreadful vulnerability of girls' sexual parts, so that they always have to be wearing knickers.

I feel that with my liberal approach I'm very much above all this. Then on our way home we stop briefly at a fairground and as we are standing by the side of the road, waiting for the lights to change, facing a crowd of people on the other side, Anneli suddenly pulls up her dress to her neck, revealing her nakedness to everyone. Panic floods through me – it's as though I was standing at this crossing naked myself, and I tell her she can't do that and order her to put her dress straight again. I don't even wait for her to react, but pull the dress down myself. She runs merrily on without making any comment. But I'm sure my behaviour must have left some impression.

So what was it all about? Why did I feel personally distressed by her nakedness? I can't understand where this enormous taboo about the naked female genitals comes from. Only today did I decide that it was passed on by the world around us, but I myself, although I felt superior when discussing it with others, reacted in exactly the same way when taken by surprise.

It would seem that there is something special about girls 'down there' and it ought to be covered up. Exhibitionism in girls makes adults panic. Exhibitionism in boys when they pee is regarded as an achievement, sometimes even encouraged, and generally felt to be quite normal.

The *6th Youth Report on Equality of Opportunity for Girls* in the FRG which was published by the government in mid-1984 says the following:

'Whereas parents and teachers tend to react to girls' showing sexual interest or proudly exposing their naked bodies with at best disregard or more commonly prohibition or punishment, most find it easy to regard comparable behaviour in boys as amusing or in general to be more tolerant . . . Girls develop little self-confidence as far as their own sexuality is concerned, since it does not seem socially acceptable. But early on boys link their activities with masculine sexuality, as a physical show of strength directed at girls. Thus by the time they go to school girls have discovered that their bodies cannot offer any protection against attack but on the contrary actually encourage it. As they grow into the role designated for them they seem to grasp that the limitations on their movements are closely connected with the sexual purpose their bodies have for others.'[15]

22 August 1983 (2 years)

Jürgen, a colleague of mine, is visiting us and we go out to an ice-cream parlour. He carries Anneli. On the way there she suddenly says 'Car broke down' and when we stop and look round, true enough, there's a car with the bonnet open. I say, 'Yes, it's being repaired,' and walk on. I don't care about the car. But Jürgen stops, then he goes over to the car, lets her look at the engine, explains the various parts and shows her how cables, pipes, etc. are connected with one another. She doesn't understand it all, of course, but her interest has been aroused. She listens with great interest and concentration and watches his hands moving from one part of the engine to another. They spend some time by this car, while I stand some way off, bored and taking no part in the explanation. Never would an open car bonnet have given me the idea of explaining all this to her. I'm ashamed when I see how interested she is because it occurs to me that I have been suppressing something that is quite an important part of life today. Have I deliberately been keeping her away from technical things?

1 September 1983 (2 years 1 month)

We are on our way back to Munich and have a passenger.* During a stop in a lay-by Anneli sees an HGV driver repairing his vehicle. She gives a cry of delight, 'Engine broke,' and runs over to have a look. I don't go with her, but our male passenger does. I don't care what's wrong with the thing. Anyway, after that first instruction

*See footnote on p 34.

from Jürgen she's already talking about an 'engine' and no longer simply saying 'Car broke.'

Once again explanations are exchanged between the driver and our passenger. I'm some distance away, so the conversation is only between men, except for Anneli.

5 September 1983 (2 years 1 month)

Back in Munich. In the afternoon Anneli notices a miniature Lamborghini on Klaus's desk. It's a very ingenious model with moving parts and she wants to have it. When I refuse, because it belongs to Klaus, she starts crying. Since it seems so important I do then give it to her. She plays with it with great interest for a long time, then she comes asking me to mend a bit of it. She asks, 'Look, Mummy, where's the engine?' and 'What's this?' and 'What's that?' She is very interested in all the parts of the car and particularly wants to see the engine. I'm at a complete loss and make something up; I feel really ignorant, a typical woman who hasn't a clue about engines, fiddling around with a model car trying to cover up my lack of knowledge. My explanations sound like a story retold by a child who hasn't quite understood it. I continually have to resist the impulse to get out of the difficulty by saying 'Ask Daddy when he comes home this evening' or by suggesting some bright idea for another game to distract her. I don't do either. But only because I have recently become aware of my own attitude to cars and am now forcing myself to stick with the subject. I want to show her that women can understand cars. This time I don't want to give her the impression that cars are men's business.

In doing this I begin to realise why women are not interested in mechanical things. Mothers' lack of interest and knowledge often discourages their daughters (compare 22 August 1983). When daughters do show any interest they get no real support from their mothers, meeting nothing but boredom and ignorance.

In the case of a boy a mother refers him to his father and interest is kept alive until Daddy has time. But with a girl the original enthusiasm dies. Mother does not regard it as a subject worth cultivating. So the first access to technology is blocked and the initial interest directed into other channels the mother understands and is familiar with. Thus, mother's and daughter's interests become identical and all women become more alike.

Now – at last – I feel that there is a challenge for me as a mother to comes to terms with technology.

The same evening Klaus is knocking out a dent in the car. He's lying on the ground, using a hammer and other necessary tools, and to a child it all looks enormously interesting and important; Anneli watches with great enthusiasm. In the meantime I'm indoors cooking. Once again the message to Anneli is clear and reinforces the cultural barrier between women and technology, which is closely linked with various physical taboos.[16]

If we envisage a woman in the same position, then the very picture conjured up puts us off: the woman, covered in oil and sweating, lying on her back under the car, legs apart, face distorted with the effort of changing an exhaust. The majority of women will, if they are honest, recoil at such an image for themselves and their daughters. And precisely because this image is *not* there, what we pass on to the girls is that technical things are not for women.

7 September 1983 (2 years 1 month)

I have to hand in a peace group poster at the local Lutheran church and cycle there with Anneli. When she asks me where we're going I automatically answer 'To the clergyman's,' although in this case the pastor is in fact a woman. So why don't I tell her so? Despite the fact that there are women in the Lutheran church my Catholic upbringing has apparently made it impossible for me to envisage a female pastor. Since she doesn't exist in the world as I spontaneously conceive it, I can't name her. When we have handed in the poster and are about to set off back Anneli says she'd like to go into the church and I tell her the clergyman has locked it up. It's only at this point – a minute after we have spoken to the woman pastor – that the penny drops, so I now explain to Anneli that the pastor is a woman, the one we've just seen. Anneli is quite contented, saying that the clergywoman has locked up because she's having her lunch.

I'm really taken aback at the difficulty I have imagining a woman in this 'man's job'. But how much did I myself suffer because of people's ignorance, when I was a female judge! How complicated I make everything for the child, concealing the truth from her for fear it could be too complicated and completely forgetting that she sees things without the conditioning I have had and is therefore quite able to accept it. It was me who was making difficulties with my own conceptual roles, slipping behind what we have already laboriously achieved. Is it surprising that roles survive from generation to generation and fit like a second skin?

16 September 1983 in the Engadine (2 years 1 month)
The three of us are sitting in the living room. Klaus is playing with her on the floor when I happen to mention that I would like a drink. Anneli says to Klaus, 'Daddy, do you want a glass of beer?' I realise from this question that it is only Klaus who drinks beer with his evening meal. For Anneli the traditional advertising link between man and beer has already been established.

We are leafing through a sketch pad we always take with us when we go on holiday. I discover all sorts of drawings that we've done over the past few months: animals, flowers, houses; then there's a drawing I did of a human figure. It's wearing trousers and a hat and above it I have written 'man'. Why didn't I draw her a woman? Does every human being that turns up have to be a man? And girls aren't supposed to learn that men always have priority when we are talking about human beings. Later on Klaus plays with the toy cars with her. I now know where the engine is and am able to give her some information in response to her questions. But I don't offer to play with the cars of my own accord. Not yet. I haven't yet learned to initiate play with things that don't interest me.

I realise that here in the Engadine Anneli has been meeting a lot of men that arouse her interest. The farmers with their tractors, the guard on the Rhätikon railway she's allowed to buy the tickets from, the bus driver with the jazzy sunglasses, the chewing gum and the fantastic motor horn. After each bus journey she can hardly bear to part from him though he doesn't deign to cast a single glance in her direction. And then all the hunters with their guns; one day we even see one of them coming down the mountain with a chamois slung across his back. I try to convince her that she can become a huntress later if she wants to, but we haven't seen any women hunting and earlier haven't so much as mentioned one.

Whilst she's getting undressed in the bathroom she says, 'I'm a boy.' When Klaus asks her whether she'd like to be a boy, she says 'Yes!' My heart sinks to my boots when I hear that.

17 September 1983 (2 years 1 month)
It's the hunting season in the Engadine and one day we see a stag being gutted at a farm. Anneli insists on being allowed to watch the whole process and gets into conversation with the Swiss family. I realise they all think she's a boy and make no attempt to put them right. She wants to see everything and have it all explained. No doubt that's why the people tell her that she'll be able to be a hunter one day and they explain what she has to do to shoot a deer. Anneli agrees and for days afterwards she says she wants to be a hunter. I'm absolutely convinced they would never have envisaged a hunting future for her if they had realised she was a girl.

We return to the flat. Ellen is waiting for us with four-year-old Martin. Anneli describes the dissection of the deer with great enthusiasm and mimes it all with grand gestures. Whereupon Ellen tells her she'll make a fine butcher's wife! Knowing she's a girl Ellen can only see Anneli as the wife of a butcher and not the butcher or the hunter themselves, unlike the locals who thought she was a boy.

20 September 1983 (2 years 1 month)
Martin goes on all the time about his fantastic Daddy, who is tall, knows and can do everything, and is so marvellous he even goes climbing in the highest mountains with snow on the top. None of the adults tells him that lots of people do that and that his mother has also been high up in the mountains, and so Martin's assertions do not meet any contradiction. His idea of the greatness of his father as compared with his mother goes unchallenged, and she certainly says nothing. Anneli listens fascinated, her glances moving from Martin to the mountain.

Since I'm sure this is not an isolated case it doesn't surprise me when an acquaintance tells me that her four-and-a-half-year-old asked her: 'Mummy, are men more important than women? Because you always ask Daddy when you want to open a tin or a jar of jam. And food's important.'

21 September 1983 (2 years 1 month)
We're having a picnic up in one of the Alpine meadows. The sausages we're eating have metal rings at the end which can't simply be slipped off. Martin wants someone to remove his. Although I'm

handing round the food and have the knife in my hand Ellen says, 'Ask Klaus, he'll do it for you.' Sometimes women seem to relinquish all idea of competence in even simple things just because there are men present and pass on the most trivial jobs to them.

Later on Martin says that when he's bigger he'll go climbing in the high mountains with his father. So I ask whether he couldn't go with his mother. He responds with an emphatic 'no', stressing that only Daddy can climb so high. Although she's very good at sports and has done a lot of climbing Ellen does not contradict him; presumably she doesn't want to seem silly and envious and has good enough reason for remaining silent.

A few days later a woman friend and I go off for three days of longer tours in the mountains; Anneli stays behind with her father. When we get back she tells us that when she grows up she's going to go climbing in the really high mountains with her Mummy and Sophie. Thanks to this one example, Anneli at least is planning her future tours with women in contrast to Martin.

24 September 1983 (2 years 1 month)
During a trip in the car Martin is talking about all the things he's going to do when he grows up. He's going to marry his girl friend, Andrea, who will then be called Andrea Huber, that is, she'll take his surname.

Klaus and Ellen, both of whom are lawyers, are in the car; both know that the woman does not have to adopt the name of her husband on marriage, but neither of them thinks to contradict or correct him and none of us points out that he'll have to ask Andrea what she thinks. The little man is already making decisions about a little woman without any modification or correction from any of us adults present. In this way the boy acquires unlimited self-confidence in his dealings with girls.

27 September 1983 (2 years 1 month)
There have been more sweet things available in the past few days than usual.

In the morning we're sitting in the bus, ready to set off on an excursion, and I look at the people around me. An attractive, delicately built young woman gets into the bus and when she smiles her pretty face becomes really beautiful. I admire her. And then I suddenly realise what a close connection there is between good teeth and an attractive and pleasing appearance in a woman and at once I resolve not to let Anneli miss cleaning her teeth after she has been eating sweets or to allow her to get out of it with her usual tricks. From now on teeth cleaning is strictly carried out. After all I do want her to look nice when she grows up.

Martin's not abused by his mother in this way. Is Anneli at the age of two already the victim of the feminine need to be beautiful?

28 September 1983 (2 years 1 month)
After comments from Klaus that I'm dressing her up too prettily I let Anneli run around in Ftan for a few days in a track suit and wellies.

This afternoon she went off with Klaus for four hours. When she returns, tearing into the room and starting to speak, I suddenly see her in her dirty, scruffy suit with different eyes – for a moment it's as though she were a boy, and I catch myself imagining her as such. And for once I don't take her straight into my arms to give her a kiss and a cuddle but let her talk, thus taking her and what she has to say more seriously than my momentary feeling.

I'm appalled when I become aware of this. If it's really like this, if we mothers do take boys more seriously from the start, then the 'atmosphere' is much richer for boys and their self-confidence is bound to seem natural.

29 September 1983 (2 years 1 month)
I have arranged to meet Barbara with her son Felix (2 months younger than Anneli). Felix is wearing dark red and dark blue. I happen to try an angora hat on Anneli that I'm knitting her; it's pale and dark blue, white, rose, lilac and grey and variously patterned. Barbara admires it and then says: 'Pity I can't put anything like that on Felix; you can dress girls much more attractively.' I ask her why and tell her how at the beginning of the century all children wore smocks until they were three years old. She is shocked and objects, 'But I couldn't put him into a dress!' Everything in her is repelled by this; for her it is inconceivable that her son should wear a smock. As a further explanation she says she doesn't want other children or adults to laugh at him.

Once again I notice the fear that boys' mothers have that people might mistake their sons for girls if they are not dressed strictly in accordance with gender expectations. For this reason certain colours (and not just pink) are quite unacceptable for boys. What is it boys' mothers are so afraid of? Why do they try so hard to avoid having their sons being taken for girls and possibly being laughed at?

After this discussion I think again about the problem of clothes for small children, that is, the need for gender specific clothing. Isn't our society much more rigid in its attitude to what is suitable for boys than for girls? Boys' mothers seem to stick to an unspoken code and avoid any form of clothing that could in any way resemble girls' or in which their sons' sex might be mistaken. Girls, on the other hand, are often seen wearing boys' clothes.

30 September 1983 (2 years 1 month)
Ellen has been to Monaco with Martin. She says that she'd heard that the maritime museum was particularly interesting and that she'd taken Martin to see it because she thought a boy was bound to find it interesting and that it was important for him to see the exhibits connected with shipping. At the same time she stresses that she would never have taken a daughter there, however interesting she had been told it was. With a girl she would have gone shopping and to a smart café.

The same old story! The daughter can make do with the things that interest the mother, but with a little man she feels obliged to show him all the wonders of the world.

1 October 1983 (2 years 2 months)
In the afternoon I go out and Grandma has come to look after Anneli. When I get back home, the doll is sitting there with its hair all nicely done and Grandma is praising Anneli for keeping her hair tidy for so long, so I guess they've been playing at doing dolly's and Anneli's hair.

A bit later Anneli takes a decorative comb she finds and puts it in her hair, saying, 'Now we go shopping and people all look at me.' No doubt she means that she wants her beauty to be admired – an idea, new to her, that no doubt she's got from Grandma.

A bit later still we're going out to see some friends and she insists, quite unlike her usual self, on having her hair done. 'Now I got to do my hair so I look pretty.' I'm amazed; this is all new to me. Usually, as soon as she catches a glimpse of me with a hair brush, trying desperately once a day to get out the worst of the tangles, she runs off and afterwards ruffles her hair with her hands.

In the evening she's at her babysitter's. When she comes back she's got a new, highly decorative, hairstyle with all sorts of clips, slides and little plaits in it. With all these curls she looks so sweet and pretty I'm quite carried away; suddenly I see in her a perfect image of myself: 'Mummy's little girl'. I really let myself go and tell her how pretty she looks. Then I take a few photographs of her and she holds herself still and stiff, so as not to disturb a single hair in the style that has produced such an effect.

If she'd been a boy I'd never have made such a fuss as this about hair and hairstyle. Just to check, a few days later I question Isabell, mother of four-and-a-half-year-old Ben. She admits to having persuaded Ben not to go to the supermarket, as he wanted, with his sister's slides in his hair, because she was afraid people would laugh at him. When she did allow him to keep them in once, when he went to the family who looked after him during the day, what she had feared did in fact happen. The father and his 13-year-old son roared with laughter and explained to Ben that men (he's four-and-a-half) did not wear things like that. The same thing happened when he turned up one day wearing nail polish.

So women and men pay meticulous attention to observing the masculine code. Ben, who is growing up in a family of women and girls, does not seem to suffer naturally from any masculinity complex. It's being taught to him for the future by men with their utter narrow-mindedness and lack of imagination.

3 October 1983 (2 years 2 months)

Anneli enjoys cutting things out. I give her the cover of a travel brochure to cut up because it's so brightly coloured. But before she starts cutting she looks at the picture on the cover carefully. It shows a holiday home; on the terrace a man and two children are sitting at a heavily laden breakfast table, while the mother hurries towards them carrying a tray of crockery. A typical family cliché; they're all laughing, the mother most of all. Anneli is not satisfied with just looking at the picture; she wants to talk to me about it. Who are these people? Why are they doing this or that? Why are the father and the children sitting down while the mother carries things in? My explanations are pathetic. Can't I so much as give her a scrap of paper to cut up without handing out the whole patriarchal family ideology? Do I have to censor everything in the house before giving her it? Once again I realise, as I did with the 'woman nothing on' episodes, what a major role advertisements, which on the whole are forced upon us and which we cannot avoid, play in maintaining our cultural identity and passing this on to our children, who perceive them as simply more pictures.

13 October 1983 (2 years 2 months)
Anneli and I are visiting Regina and her son, Sebastian, who is a month younger than Anneli. Our conversation is almost exclusively about children. Among other things Regina tells us about Sebastian's toy toolbox, with hammer, pliers and nails made of wood, which he loves playing with. At the same time she tells us that he can also knock nails in with a real hammer; he taught himself that. Apart from whether a child of this age is able to use a proper hammer and nails, what interested me was the fact that already, before his second birthday, the boy was shown tools and given suitable toys for them. It had never occurred to me to do this with Anneli; apart from her little bench I had never thought of giving her tools. But this is now an incentive for me to abandon my mother–daughter ignorance as far as tools are concerned (that is, what means nothing to me means nothing to my daughter).

So off we go to a DIY shop and Anneli and I decide to buy her a little screwdriver. She's enormously proud of it, heads straight for her bike and begins to 'repair' it. Whilst we're standing there an assistant from the store joins us. 'Well, laddie,' he says, 'so you're mending your bike yourself already; that's great, and you've got a screwdriver as well. You'll be needing that for your handiwork. You'll soon be mending things for Mummy at home and when you grow up you can be a car mechanic.'

I wonder what he'd have said if Anneli had been wearing a skirt and recognisable as a girl? I doubt he'd have got as far as the bit about the car mechanic.

We cycle next to the stationer's to buy some children's scissors. Anneli proudly shows her screwdriver to the sales assistant. Having asked her name and thus ascertained her sex, the woman says sceptically, 'I hope you're as handy with a needle and thread – or were you intending to be a mechanic when you grow up?'

20 October 1983 (2 years 2 months)

We are staying with a friend and her four-year-old son in the country. Living as we do on a farm we don't bath the children every evening.

One day, when we're frolicking with the children in the meadow, romping and rolling about in the grass and embracing one another so that bodily contact is close, my friend says – in front of the children – 'You know, little girls somehow have a funny smell down there; I have noticed it in his [her son's] little girl friends and I notice it with Anneli. Somehow they smell funny. That's not the case with boys, or I haven't noticed it; they don't smell at all.'

Has the work of Theodor Reik – whom my friend has probably never read – and his misogynistic ideas become so widespread that we're influenced by them without realising it? He explains the origins of cleanliness in women as follows: 'I believe that cleanliness has a double origin: the first in the taboos of tribes, and the second another matter coming thousands of years later, namely in women's awareness of their own odour, specifically the bad smells caused by the secretions of their genitals.'[17]

Has patriarchy actually changed our sense of smell? Can we only understand a woman as a being that naturally produces evil smells, whilst we don't so much as notice the pong of a penis that hasn't been washed for several days? Maybe it's because we were told as little girls we smelt funny.

25 October 1983 (2 years 2 months)

We drive into Munich to pick Klaus up from work. Our conversation revolves around Daddy's work and Anneli says he works in an office. Then she asks me whether I have an office as well. I explain that I haven't got one at the moment but that, when she gets bigger, I'll go back to work and then I'll have one as well. She says, 'Then you'll go to work and be the Daddy and Klaus will stay at home with me.' So work is connected with the father figure. But at the same time Daddy also means man.

Something in the traffic attracts her attention and she asks, 'Why is that man driving like that?' I reply that it might just as well be a woman because we can't tell the sex of the driver. People she doesn't know, whose sex is not clear, are defined as men. Has Anneli already adopted the masculine primacy of our language?

Anneli and her friends have been showing a lot of interest in the police recently. But we only ever see policemen. I'm eagerly waiting to see a policewoman at the wheel of a police car.

In town we see some writing on an enormous poster and she asks, 'Which man wrote that?' Once again I point out that it might have been a woman.

26 October 1983 (2 years 2 months)

We're visiting the house of a woman with a four-year-old son. I've heard her say how she likes to see little girls in pretty dresses and without really thinking I have put on Anneli her one and only dress, which she has inherited from another child. Only in the evening does it occur to me that I have, against my better intentions, dressed Anneli in feminine clothing just to please someone else. She was accordingly admired. Boys don't get this sort of training.

My acquaintance tells us about a house warming party she had been to and expresses horror because the house had white fitted carpets, although the owners had a small child. But in almost the same breath she qualifies this, saying, 'But then, the child's a girl and it's easier to teach girls to be clean than boys. Boys are such hopeless mudlarks. I don't know why, but all the girls the same age as my son are a lot cleaner.'

Maybe the secret of this puzzle is to be found in the words 'teach' with girls and 'hopeless' in boys? Perhaps it is in the belief that boys are simply like that, with the result that their teaching is less intensive?

At a neighbour's in the evening Anneli's dress is once again admired. I can tell that already the dress is no longer simply an article of clothing; it makes people admire her.

2 November 1983 (2 years 3 months)

I want to make pear juice with my new juice extractor, but it doesn't work as I thought it did. When I can't find the instructions I get ratty and mutter 'Bloody machines.' Anneli is standing next to me, listening. Klaus comes home from the office. I explain the problem to him and ask him to repair it, which he does. Anneli watches, annoyed, because she is waiting to play with Daddy. In a few minutes the wretched thing is working – all that was wrong was that it wasn't standing straight!

Another perfect example for Anneli of how things are: woman and gadget don't get on; Daddy's help is sought; it's repaired and everything's okay.

This behaviour once again gives an unspoken message to children and it's well learned. Technicalities turn girls right off, but they really appeal to boys. With one group there's no interest; with the other it's a lesson in personal identification.

7 November 1983 (2 years 3 months)

We've planned an excursion. Anneli and Schorschi are already sitting in the car, but it won't start. I know what's wrong, because it's happened several times recently: the carburettor's blocked. I also know that putting it right is easy and only takes a few moments. But I can't do it because until now it never seemed worth learning. So I explain to the children, 'Car kaput, all out, phone Klaus, Daddy'll see to it.'

Klaus comes home in his lunch hour after instructions over the phone have failed and I've discovered that since I can't even recognise individual engine parts by name I'm completely snookered.

The children stand watching my unsuccessful efforts; they also stand watching Klaus get the car to start in five minutes. They are experiencing a classic division of roles. In the meantime I've been in the kitchen cooking. The whole episode has really needled me and the next time I'll be able to repair it myself. It's a lot easier than cooking.

Why, I wonder, has my resistance to working with the car and repairing it been so great? I think I was most put off by the thought of getting oil, rust and grease all over my hands and possibly of hurting myself, however slightly. It was for me a completely new sort of dirt. After all I'm familiar enough with the dirt of washing up, cleaning, nappies, the garden, painting, sick children, and all this can be pretty revolting sometimes. So why does dirt in the form of oil, grease and rust seem to be men's business? Theoretically, of course, I would have denied that I did feel like this and said it all didn't apply to me. But one concrete example, the thought of getting hold of a greasy engine, showed me the truth.

Is is because women, with few little-known exceptions, have no real share in the development of technology by means either of their own inventions or their share in economic power? Is it because technology, which is supposed to be objective, is in fact anything but? Is in fact characterised and limited by being both the creation of, and possession of, men? Technology can materially and historically be defined as being masculine. As it now is it has no application that is either female or gender neutral. We were and are turned away from it, and for that very reason perhaps we refuse to do any more than observe its function or to show any real interest in it.[18]

To change all this we, the present generation of mothers, have to make technology our concern, to strip it of its unfamiliarity. We have to force ourselves upon it and make it female friendly, so that it will be naturally accessible to our daughters. My idea that I could make technology more accessible to Anneli by giving her a screwdriver, a hammer and other 'technical' toys without *doing it myself* was naïve.

10 November 1983 (2 years 3 months)

It strikes me today that Anneli has recently increasingly been en-quiring about the 'woman's husband'; somehow she has grasped the social link between woman and man. The next question is then about the woman's children.

She also asks the surnames of all the fathers, mothers and chil-dren she knows about and discovers that father, mother and chil-dren all have the same name – except us. Thank goodness she spares me the question of why it's different in our case.

I find myself becoming both angry and depressed in response to questions as to why Felix, Martin, Schorschi, etc. all have the sur-names they do. I find it hard to answer, 'That's their Daddy's surname and so the children are called that too,' although it's the only explana-tion. Just now I find it particularly absurd when I see every day how children make work almost exclusively for women, when I see that women have not only 'made' children physically but also physically keep them alive from hour to hour. Children are almost exclusively the product of women. And women are lost in the process, since what remains is the name of the father and his sons. And this goes on through all generations – our names are cast aside and forgotten.

What effect does it have on a two-year-old girl to discover that Daddy's name is the only one for the whole family and that Mummy

Gender values handed on through names (handwritten)

hasn't got a name of her own? What effect does it have on a boy, or young man? This seems to me to be one of the many insidious ways in which gender values are handed on.

Greater self-confidence is not innate in boys! Nor modesty, reserve and insecurity in girls.

11 November 1983 (2 years 3 months)
When we are out walking someone runs past us and smiles at Anneli. The person is of medium height, rather plump, has short hair and is unfashionably dressed in black trousers and a dark jacket. Anneli stops, looks after the figure, and says, 'Is that a man or a woman?'

When appearance is completely neutral (and I wasn't able to decide the sex either) Anneli apparently has difficulties. She seems to know what women and men are supposed to look like in order to be recognised. But she does at least ask whether it might be a woman.

Felix is at our house with his mother, who tells Anneli that Felix's father has got a tool he can repair everything with and that Felix has been helping him. Felix chatters on excitedly about repairing things. Anneli doesn't show much interest and remains very reserved on the topic. Why? Just like a girl?

Neither Klaus nor I have ever asked her to help us repair things and there has been neither praise nor emphasis on this topic. I think the conclusion is obvious. Once again I realise that Klaus and I have been behaving completely in accordance with gender expectation, simply by doing nothing. Through our manner and behaviour we have made choices for her by excluding her.

In the evening she comes back from the babysitter's with a big doll and goes through all the new games with it that Tini has shown her.

12 November 1983 (2 years 3 months)
Grandma is visiting us. The weather's bad so Anneli can't go to the playground. But Grandma always thinks of something and they play at doing the doll's hair and at dressing and undressing her. After an hour and a half of intense effort Anneli has learned several new things about the outer appearance of girls – the doll is, of course, a girl.

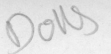

18 November 1983 (2 years 3 months)

I visit a group of friends living together, where there are two small boys (two and four years old). The mother of the older boy complains that her son only wants to play with cars and aeroplanes and not with the doll she has recently bought him.

Boys' mothers often cite the dolls they have bought their sons as proof of the unbiased approach they have to child rearing. At the same time the rejection or lack of interest in the doll is quoted as proof that certain forms of behaviour are typical and natural in boys.

So I ask whether Sebastian ever had a doll before, whether Grandma, his mother or babysitter have ever played with him with a doll. The mother laughs and says they haven't. The question amuses her: 'What, give him a doll even earlier? But he only played with cars, anyway. And I don't want to play with dolls with him. You see, if he doesn't want to play with a doll then I'm not going to force him. I don't want to be domineering with him. How would he get on at kindergarten and with other children if he suddenly spent all his time with the girls among the dolls? They might all just laugh at him.'

We continue to talk about this and that. Then she begins to praise her son's craft work and explains how good he is at it. Since she guesses how I react to gender specific upbringing she also says that he occasionally helps her with the cooking and that she will sometimes stick a duster in his hand. These things are related and praised at length, all within the boy's hearing. He must get the impression that it's something really special when he helps with the cooking.

20 November 1983 (2 years 3 months)

Anneli takes a record of a Schubert symphony out and wants to play it because she likes the sleeve so much. Then she enquires, 'Which man is it playing?' I just manage to choke back the answer 'Someone I don't know' and instead point out that it might just as well be a woman. So then she asks me the woman's name. I invent a woman's name. The extent to which she already accepts the masculine principle still bothers me. (Only later, on 18 September 1984, does the connection become clear.)

We go and see Schorschi. For the first time I notice that his doll has got a penis – if you have to give a boy a doll make sure it's male!

27 November 1983 (2 years 3 months)

Klaus and I have a row. We argue in the kitchen, whilst Anneli sits in the dining room waiting for her dinner. I started the argument and I fairly let rip. So does he. And then in the middle of the argument I burst into tears out of sheer fury. During the meal Anneli tries to console me, asking, 'Why did Daddy tell you off?'

I'm really annoyed at the effect my tears have had on her and try to explain that I was also telling Daddy off, but she disregards this explanation and sticks to her statement that I was the one being scolded. She feels that because I cried I was the weaker party, the one who could be rebuked, and in reacting like this she is trans-ferring her own experience to the relationship between men and women. Since she cries when I tell her off, and she is the weaker person in our relationship, then automatically the person who scolds must be in the right, that is, the stronger. Tears for the child are a sign of inferiority, of weakness, of having to obey. Ellen tells me that Martin reacts to similar situations with the question as to why Daddy is telling her off.

I recall my own childhood. When my parents quarrelled I always felt my mother's weakness and sympathised with her. At moments like this my father always seemed threatening, angry and strong, able to humble my mother, a person it was better not to make angry.

This shows that the existing power relations between men and women are already clear at an early age (two-and-a-half), partly because a woman tends more readily to express anger and sadness through tears. This similarity between woman and child in the physical reaction of crying is one of the reasons why the child compares the social status of the woman to its own. From that girls can deduce their own value, boys that of the girls and women they know.

I feel as though I've discovered an important reason why women feel inferior.

28 November 1983 (2 years 3 months)

We have been invited to Felix's second birthday party. I wonder what to take him as a present and decide that Anneli really ought to

Boxes for reactions
B + g.

give him one of her toys, because that would be a real present from
her. And what do I think of? A toy motorbike, for in *my*(!) opinion
Anneli, on the one hand, has had too many toys like this given her
by a neighbour and, on the other, doesn't play with them as much
as Felix, who is always surrounded by cars. I ask Anneli 'Would
you like to give Felix that motorbike? He likes playing with toys
like that.' She agrees; she doesn't care for it much.

So first of all a boy is given cars because he's a boy, and then
he's given more because he likes playing with them so much. It's
not until the evening that I see my own part in all this.

At the party there is a boy of about the same age called Tim. He
is very reserved, shy and rather small in comparison to the other
boys there. His clothes are quite neutral: jeans and a red pullover.
I realise that for quite some time I'm rather put out at not being
able to tell the sex of the child at first glance. To me he wasn't
immediately recognisable as a boy, and I interpret my feeling of
uncertainty as an inability deep down to regard a child neutrally.
Not only that, I am not able to enter into contact with a child in a
way that is not related to gender. There seem to be two little boxes
I take my reactions out of, one for girls and one for boys.

29 November 1983 (2 years 3 months)
Felix, a month younger than Anneli, is visiting us. The two children are running round Anneli's rocking horse in opposite direc-
tions in time to music. They bump into one another three times.
The next time Felix still runs straight ahead; Anneli gives way so
that from now on there are no more collisions. And so it goes on:
he runs straight ahead and she gives way. We two mothers look on
and say nothing. I feel quite wretched. It reminds me of the results
of experiments carried out by women,[19] of tests I've done myself
and of some a woman friend in Berlin did, that is, trying in a busy
street not always to give way to men. If the woman does not give
way in good time there is inevitably a collision.

For whatever reason Anneli in the same situation has made a
social adaptation to his advantage. She's the one who thinks ahead,
who solves a problem for both of them, who adapts her behaviour
to his.

We two mothers just take it for granted. Somehow I can't get up
the courage or the imagination to intervene and to encourage Felix

to behave differently. His mother simply doesn't notice. Once again the boy and his behaviour are accepted; the mother does not tell him to adapt to the girl but on the contrary takes the girl's behaviour for granted.

6 December 1983 (2 years 4 months)
Another year has passed. St Nicholas Day is upon us again and four children are waiting. All of them, two girls and two boys, are a little timid. Then Thomy, the eldest, is persuaded to come forward with the comment, 'Come on, a boy can't be scared of St Nicholas.' Thomy feels he's being forced to do something, as is obvious from his expression, but he does as he's told. He's a boy.

Both boys, by the way, are wearing their everyday clothes, that is, track suit or jeans and pullover. But Hanna is wearing a dress and I have put Anneli in her best blouse, with embroidery and frills, and new trousers. You can tell there's a celebration this afternoon from the girls' clothes, but not from the boys'. I had discussed it beforehand with Anneli and told her we would dress up nicely today because St Nicholas was going to bring the presents at last.

In the morning she said to me quite suddenly, 'I'm so small, I haven't got a baby yet.' And just like the mother who always has a ready answer, I'm on the point of responding, 'But you'll have one when you grow up.' But then I say nothing, as it occurs to me that the urgent need to have children that is felt by most women is perhaps due in part to an abundance of such early projections of their future.

7 December 1983 (2 years 4 months)
Klaus and I have another argument. I raise my voice again and become quite heated, but I don't cry this time. Klaus, however, is rather restrained and doesn't say much. This time Anneli says to me, 'Mummy, why are you telling Daddy off?'

A friend tells me about the Christmas presents she's bought. She has bought her neighbour's six-year-old son a model aeroplane construction set for him and his father to use together. I ask her whether she would ever give a girl a present like that. Her answer is a definite no.

8 December 1983 (2 years 4 months)
Anneli's at a friend's building three towers with Duplo bricks.
One is very high, one medium, one small. Then she announces
that they are Daddy, Mummy and baby towers.

Her father and I are both the same height. For Anneli the concept 'big' does not mean size that can be measured in centimetres,
but also ability, authority, age and importance.

14 December 1983 (2 years 4 months)
I go out for a walk with Anneli and Schorschi. She positions herself in front of a tree, legs apart and hands in front of her sexual
organs, and looks at him. I ask her what she's doing; she looks
embarrassed, doesn't answer and runs away. I ask her again
whether she's having a pee like a boy. She answers, 'No, like the
man yesterday.' (For her, yesterday means any time in the past.)

I don't quite know how to interpret her behaviour, but I think
she's embarrassed imitating something she had originally attributed to a man, something she defines as masculine behaviour. But it
must have interested her somehow, if it's occupying her in her
play. In any case I infer from it that children of her age have
already seen men relieving themselves in public and that this is
part of the atmosphere that makes men more important than
women. It's inconceivable that Anneli would ever see a woman
relieving herself in public. Men apparently don't have so much to
hide, no reason to be embarrassed, but women do . . . don't they?
Even here, the public sphere has been taken over by men.

19 December 1983 (2 years 4 months)
During a car drive Anneli suddenly asks whether witches are bad
women. I have never previously spoken to her about witches, not
even in stories, so she must have picked it up from some older
child. Off the cuff I might easily have said yes, and then I suddenly
remember all the books I've read about witches; surely I know a
bit better about what turned women into witches.[20] So I hold back
my 'yes' and explain to her that witches are clever women, who
can cure many illnesses because they know a lot about herbs that
grow in the woods and mountains and that they can help people, so
that children need not be afraid of witches because they are kind.
And then Anneli herself embroiders the story a bit and they turn

out to be really nice women. In the next few days we play witches a lot, with me asking her to give me a herb for my tummy ache and she being the witch and helping me.

Once again I'm surprised with the ease with which I was, against my better knowledge, going to pass on to my daughter a patriarchal lie about women. Without the awareness this diary gives me I would have told her the old stories, even though I've actually been to *Walpurgisnacht* demonstrations myself.

In the evening I'm taking the crockery out of the dishwasher and she wants to help me put the plates in the wall cupboards. I take them from her, saying she isn't big enough yet. She is offended and replies, 'But when I grow bigger and I'm a boy, then I'll be able to do it as well.'

I can hardly believe my ears. To her being special, being big, is the same as being a boy. I don't know where she's got it from, but obviously my daughter believes that if she were a boy she'd be able to do a lot more.

20 December 1983 (2 years 4 months)
Klaus and I are going to a concert and Grandma comes to babysit. Anneli feels there's something special in the air and asks what a concert is. I answer, 'A lot of people sit in a large beautiful room and listen to other people playing music, piano, flute, violin, guitar.' I mention all the instruments she knows.

'Are they all men?' she asks. To me an orchestra – not only in my imagination but to some extent in reality – is composed principally of men, but I manage not simply to say 'yes', but tell her that women and men play together and that women can play beautiful music.

In the concert hall I count the orchestra: two women and 25 men. Have I told her a lie?

21 December 1983 (2 years 4 months)
In the afternoon we've been with Barbara and Felix to a gymnastics class for mothers and children. On the way we're talking about the police and the fire brigade. Both the children show the same amount of interest. I don't react much to this discussion but Barbara says to Felix, 'Tomorrow I'll take you to the fire station and we can look at everything there carefully – then you'll be able to see the big fire engines and the ladders.'

The idea of taking Anneli to the fire station would never have occurred to me. Is this another case of a girl's mother taking her child less seriously than boys' mothers? I don't mean that it's intentional, but just due to thoughtlessness, convenience, simple ignorance and lack of respect for the little girl's interests. Boys' mothers, on the other hand, feel obliged, because the child is not the same sex as themselves, to overcome their own limitations. It's respect for the growing man plus acceptance of the cliché that boys are more interested in the big wide world.

23 December 1983 (2 years 4 months)

Anneli and I pay a pre-Christmas visit to an aunt and uncle of mine. Their grandchild, Maximilian, who is a year older than Anneli, happens to be there at the same time. Lots of toys are laid out on the big table in the living room, including a big lorry. Anneli goes straight over to it, plays with it with great interest and enthusiasm. When Maximilian wants his toy back and Anneli is reluctant to part with it, his grandfather comforts him, saying, 'Let Anneli play with it; after all she's a girl and girls don't have toys like that at home to play with. They've only(!) got dolls and little prams and toy kitchens.' A little later, when a similar conflict arises on account of some other object, his grandfather says, 'Be a gentleman, let her play with it, after all she's a girl.'

These comments begin to niggle me; I don't like them. There seems to me to be a connection between his grandfather's appeal to the sense of chivalry of the three-and-a-quarter-year-old boy towards Anneli, because of her sex, and the general estimation and seriousness given to women and girls. The very tone of voice, which is difficult to describe but with which all women are familiar, makes it clear that Anneli is not really an equal partner but something different, that is, a girl. Since girls haven't got anything sensible to play with at home anyway, it's all right to be magnanimous towards them. She is certainly not an equal competitor in the squabbles about the lorry.

At home a parcel has arrived for Anneli from Grandma Rosner in Berlin. What's in it? A doll dressed as a girl with long feminine hair. Two days later one of our neighbours gives Anneli a doll she's made herself, with beautiful long blonde hair. Two weeks later in Berlin she'll get a late present of a sweet old-fashioned doll with a frilly night-cap. Last year and the year before (her first Christmas) she was given dolls by both her grandmas.

24 December 1983 (2 years 4 months)

Today Anneli has her bath in the afternoon. As soon as she's in the water she spreads her legs as usual and pees. Grandma, who is bathing her, says, 'Hey, do you think you're Schorschi, doing a weewee standing up? You're not a little boy.' Grandma clearly doesn't know that in fact Schorschi crouches down. She seems to think masculine behaviour is worse than the fact that Anneli is piddling into her own bath water, which she's not really keen on, either.

After her bath and before she sees the presents* she is dressed in her only white blouse and tights and her little pinafore dress – all presents from friends. She does have nicer trousers, but of course on Christmas Eve she has to wear the clothes Mummy connects with festive occasions, that is, feminine clothes. My feelings and ideas about celebrations and women's clothes, which after all have gone through 36 years of patriarchal brain washing, are applied to my daughter as well. And now I remember a passage from Orwell's *1984*. Orwell puts the following words into the mouth of his heroine: 'Yes, dear, scent too. And do you know what I'm going to do next? I'm going to get hold of a real woman's frock from somewhere and wear it instead of these bloody trousers. I'll wear silk stockings and high-heeled shoes! In this room I'm going to be a woman, not a Party comrade.'[21] My goddess! If that's what makes us women, then our femininity really is in a bad way. And that's what I'm passing on to my daughter. But on the other hand I do want her to have some feeling for celebrations and for beauty. How then?

Two well meant intentions conflict here and it all seems too confused to me; that one can only be solved to the detriment of the other.

I think that the choice that a girl has between trousers and skirt or dress is an advantage, one of the very few she has that men don't. Sometimes I wonder what is so awful about dresses that their sexist character has become the subject of so many theories.[22]

---

*In Germany Christmas presents – presumed to have been brought by the infant Jesus – are laid out under the Christmas tree on Christmas Eve. (*Translator's note*.)

Of course, the fact that as an article of clothing a dress is connected with the definition of a girl is one of the things against it. As a saleswoman in the supermarket put it yesterday, when she was corrected by Anneli for addressing her as a 'lad', 'Well, how do you expect anyone to know you're a girl if you don't wear a dress?' Just as with Orwell, it's the dress that makes the girl, not the sex. The knowledge of the sex of a child influences the way it's treated, as we have seen several times. For girls this means all sorts of restrictions, the most simple being limitation on freedom of movement. A neighbour of mine once scolded me for taking her daughter (four-and-a-half) to the playground. 'She can't go to the adventure playground when she's got white tights and a skirt on, she might catch a cold or get dirty.' But that's only one mother's comment, and we can put our girls in trousers. A little girl ought to be able to do everything a little boy can do. That at least is a start towards giving girls real equality of opportunity. So what more do we want?

What seems to me questionable is that ideas of beauty that are linked to festive occasions require women to look feminine without any comparable changes being demanded of boys' behaviour in their development of aesthetic sensitivity. Boys go on wearing the colours reserved for them: dark blue, brown, grey and green. I pity them. Standing in the department store at a socks counter for three- to four-year-olds, all of them in these glum colours, I understand why boys have so little feeling for beauty. As long as boys are not able to dress in the same bright colours as girls, to adorn themselves as girls do, and this not only at home but also when they go 'out', then the pleasures of selection will, for women, continue to remain a duty.

A woman remains chained to her feminine beauty. But I don't think we should abandon it; we need *more* beauty and have to extend it to include boys and men. Let boys start wearing pink at last.

26 December 1983 (2 years 4 months)
I'm summing up after Christmas. Anneli's Christmas presents were two dolls, a stuffed animal, a small Duplo set, a book of fairy tales and an ivory necklace. Schorschi got a wooden railway, a live rabbit, several Duplo sets with a filling station and a dredger, etc.,

and, jointly with his seven-year-old sister, a toy shop. Felix got several large cars and lorries, an enormous collection of Duplo with all sorts of gadgets and figures and a picture book by Mitgutsch.[23]

I'm not quite sure whether my real reason for not giving Anneli all the Duplo dredgers, planes, lorries, etc. is that I don't want to overwhelm her too early with all the plastic and technology of our culture or whether I'm somehow influenced by the fact she's a girl. Am I perhaps more easily convinced by anthroposophical arguments because she's a girl? Wouldn't I somewhere deep down have a bad conscience if she were a boy? A friend of mine said, 'It'll be strange later on for a boy when he goes to a playgroup if he's never had the toys other boys are familiar with and wants to play with the girls.' Another case of boys' mothers being afraid that experiments with education could damage their sons so much that they won't achieve a 'masculine identity' and therefore face problems in this 'man's world'? These fears are genuine.

A six-year-old girl who has very conservative parents is visiting us. We are talking about her local playmates. She tells us that no one wants to play with Gunni (a boy) 'because he plays with dolls'. The girls won't play with him because he's a boy, the boys because he plays like a girl.

28 December 1983 (2 years 4 months)
Anneli is playing with the Duplo pieces she got for Christmas and realises that one of the building units is a dredger. Now she needs a 'dredger man' to go with it. Klaus suggests that she use the figure of the girl as it would do just as well and hands her it. She rejects it with exasperation. 'That's a girl.'

Klaus: 'Can't girls drive dredgers?'

Anneli: 'No, because women would get their hands dirty then.'

I'm shocked but recognise my own dislike of the grease, oil and dirt involved in car repairs (compare 2 November 1983).

I'm sure I never actually said as much and am inclined to think she got this from Grandma. Or was my behaviour itself enough to lead her to this conclusion? I can hardly believe so.

29 December 1983 (2 years 4 months)
On our way to the car we see a man in a wheelchair and Anneli

wants to know why he is sitting in it. I tell her a story about a car accident, the hospital the man was sent to and how he cried because he couldn't walk any more.

Her response: 'But Daddies don't cry.' To her, 'Daddy' is the same as 'man'.

I: 'Why?'

She: 'No, Mummy, Daddies don't cry; only Mummies and children cry.'

I don't say any more, but a couple of hours later she begins again, 'But Mummy, Daddies can't cry.' I respond by telling her that Daddies can cry, to which she replies, 'Not my Daddy.'

That's true; she's never seen her father cry. She has seen me cry, she has seen friends of mine cry, she has seen Grandma cry, she has seen other children cry – but never a man, not one of her friends' fathers.

2 January 1984 (2 years 5 months)

I realise that it gets on my nerves a bit to see how long and with what enthusiasm Anneli can play with her dolls without me ever having encouraged her to do so (or so I imagine). She wants me to join in, but I refuse. I don't want to get involved with the obviously 'girlish' aspects of her games and I make my irritation apparent by refusing.

But why can't I simply let her be to play as she wants? If the child was previously brought up to be a girl, does she now have to become a boy for fear of falling into traditional feminine behaviour patterns? Obviously, regardless of which point of view a mother has, whether conservative or emancipatory, the girl is always being directed. I am very annoyed with myself, because that's not what I want, either.

3 January 1984 (2 years 5 months)

During our evening meal Anneli once again says, 'Daddies can't cry, can they Mummy?'

I tell her, 'Ask Daddy.'

She: 'Do Daddies cry? How do Daddies cry then?' Then she makes Klaus show her how he cries. She enjoys this and so she asks how each of the men she knows cries and Klaus shows her, without any real tears, of course.

Satisfied, she turns to me, 'Mummy, how does Elizabeth cry, does she cry like you, Mummy?' This is a rhetorical question, just for confirmation, for she has already seen Elizabeth cry.

Since she has never seen a man cry Anneli assumes that it must be different. Thus she makes a clear distinction, for she has seen how much the behaviour of men and women varies in other respects. So it seems likely that this is also the case with crying.

And Klaus is demonstrating a lie, for he and several of the other men he represents in fact never do cry.

5 January 1984 (2 years 5 months)
In the morning we sit at the piano for a while, singing and tinkling a little. We have her collection of children's songs open at 'Sleep baby sleep' in front of us. The music and words are on the left hand side and on the right are accompanying pictures: a shepherd, sheep, trees and the moon, all the subjects of the song – except one.

Anneli asks, 'Where's the Mummy?'

And it's true; there's no mother anywhere to be seen. It's a good example of what I had been reading recently in the typescript of a book of the representation, or rather non-existence, of women in picture books.[24] I was surprised when I read in it that the number of male and female characters, the appearance of heroic figures, could have such a decisive influence and was inclined to assume that children didn't really notice this. With her obvious question Anneli has taught me better. Why portray the sheep, I wonder, rather than the woman? Yet another example of that thoughtlessness which helps create a general atmosphere in which women are less important, not even worth including in a picture along with the sheep!

In the evening we leave for Berlin. Arriving at night I stand outside the flat with Anneli in my arms, unable to open the door because something seems to be sticking. I run back downstairs to Klaus in the car to tell him. Anneli comforts me, saying 'Daddy'll see to it.'

While Klaus spends about 20 minutes fiddling around with the door we sit on the staircase watching (it's 2 a.m.). Klaus is just going to give up and try ringing some locksmith when the door suddenly swings open of its own accord. It could have happened to me just as easily – but no, to all appearances and for Anneli, it was Daddy who managed it. Even the door's against me, and Daddy has once again succeeded in mending something.

7 January 1984 (2 years 5 months)

Anneli and a friend of mine are playing with rag dolls. Anneli arranges a scene as follows: she is the baby and is lying in bed, Mummy is cleaning and tidying up, and Daddy is doing the cooking. At first I'm surprised at this scenario, but then I remember a book in which a family of mice is depicted in this way. She had been looking at it in a bookshop with two other children the day before.

So now I understand. But isn't it interesting how quickly a story from a book can have an influence and how the contents stick in a child's mind? So it is obviously critical which books and stories children have, and not something which is harmless and irrelevant.

8 January 1984 (2 years 5 months)

I notice that when Anneli is talking she always only uses masculine possessive pronouns and adjectives. Why hasn't she learned to do exactly the opposite and use feminine forms? I wonder about this and get a clear answer from the linguist Senta Trömel-Plötz, who explains that Anneli is simply internalising the masculine dominance of the German language (she says, for example, 'Anneli, *his* Mummy'). So it happens this early.

I'm having my period and since Anneli always follows me into the loo she saw the blood. In the evening I play squash with a friend; Anneli comes with me and when we're sitting around afterwards announces, 'Mummy is a little piggy, Sophie, 'cos she's got blood in her pants.'

Sophie, who is in some respects rather self-conscious, turns turkey red and immediately looks at the men sitting around to see if any of them have overheard. I waver between an appalled injunction to Anneli against saying such things and laughter at how right she is. But I can't help glancing around as well and try to change the subject. I'm sure Anneli is aware of our embarrassment.

And I have to admit that it does get on my nerves a bit that even on the days when I have my period I'm not able to sit privately in the lavatory and change my tampons without continually having to answer questions about the blood on my bottom. It does feel like an intrusion into the most private part of me. Sometimes I have to try really hard to be equal to the unselfconscious way that Anneli has, to convince myself that there's nothing wrong with her watching. I also try to explain to her that all women bleed and that there's nothing wrong with it, that it's quite normal. But after this incident at squash I find myself trying to arrange my visits to the lavatory in such a way that she's absorbed in something else or doesn't notice; I kid myself I use the tampons so quickly that she doesn't see them. But then she surprises me with the question as to whether a tampon pricks or hurts. I assure her it doesn't and tell her it's like Babylax (a children's suppository).* She remembers that because of the connection between chocolate, constipation and relief. So in spite of my secretiveness she didn't miss a thing and I'm sure she's also been aware of my attempts to conceal it. In the bath this evening she plays around with her dummy and her 'hole', as she calls it, and says, 'Just like Mummy.' She did that once before, about a year ago. She's a lot less self-conscious about it than I am.

Aren't I making a taboo of all this with my secretiveness? Am I on the point of passing on to her the same inhibitions which I unconsciously – precisely because the subject was never mentioned – picked up from my own mother? We weren't particularly prudish at home but this was a topic which simply did not exist. I only remember my mother fiddling around with cotton wool and sanitary pads, quickly and silently, and I also remember, now above all, that I understood the embarrassment in her actions and realised something was going on we couldn't talk about and which the family wasn't supposed to see. So we ourselves feel shame, especially towards men, about our own blood. A girl is embarrassed at puberty by something she has never seen, something no one has ever told her she needs to be ashamed of, not in so many words. But she is ashamed, nevertheless, not just during puberty, but as a woman for the rest of her life.

I never believed I would pass on a message like this to my

---

*A number of children's ailments in Germany are normally treated with suppositories, these being felt to be potentially less harmful than drugs. (*Translator's note.*)

daughter. I would have denied it vehemently – but it's happened, in spite of myself. I simply can't overcome these ingrained attitudes.

The *6th Youth Report* had the following to say on this subject:

> 'Even today the prevailing tendency seems to be to see as fate this monthly repeated process, which is supposed to be kept invisible and go unnoticed [compare advertising of the feminine hygiene industry]; this makes it difficult to develop a sense of confidence in one's own body, the most important element in a positive sexual identity.'[25]

9 January 1984 (2 years 5 months)

Anneli is still preoccupied with the question of Daddies crying. We're sitting in the bus when out of the blue she asks, 'Can Daddies cry?' Once again I say they can and ask her why she thinks Daddies can't cry. Her answer, 'Because they're so big.' I respond to this by telling her that Mummies are also big; she ignores this and merely repeats her previous statement.

We're in the toy department of a large store. I stop in front of a railway set on display (a plastic, not particularly nice, one) and want to stimulate her interest in it. There's no response, and I myself am not so sure what's so good about it and am quite prepared to understand her lack of interest. After a few minutes I abandon my attempt at playing railways; it seems to me pretty boring to keep pressing a button and watching the thing belt round. I can't think of anything to tell her on the subject of plastic model railways and so we move on. We arrive at a doll's house; Anneli is delighted and plays for a whole hour with the objects of her daily life, without me joining in at all. This bores me as well, but I stay with her the whole time and don't attempt to interrupt or tempt her with something else.

10 January 1984 (2 years 5 months)

Back in Berlin, we visit Isabell and exchange stories about Christmas. Isabell tells me that Ben's dearest wish was to be allowed to wear a dress or a skirt on Christmas Eve, like all the other members of the family. Previously Isabell had not allowed him to do this, but at Christmas he didn't want to be an outsider any longer. He wanted to wear the same clothes as the dominant personalities in his immediate environment, that is, his mother and older sisters. Even now Isabell resisted, as she explains with a laugh, but because it seemed to be so important to Ben, in the end she let him. It was Christmas, and after all only the family was there.

When asked why she had blocked the boy's wish to wear a dress for so long and why she had found it so difficult, she said, 'Just imagine the conflict it would create for Ben if I allowed him to run around in girls' clothes outside the house. It's the same as with the hair slides and the nail varnish. He'd simply be laughed at, hurt and made so unsure that he'd be sexually confused and possibly emotionally damaged. And I don't want that to happen, although I personally don't think it matters if a boy wears a skirt or a dress.'

It seems to me that the boy's confusion would be caused by the reaction of people around him and not by the clothing itself. Why is there no fear of a girl becoming sexually confused if she wears trousers? No doubt partly because trousers are a sign of increased prestige, and partly because sexual confusion in a girl, if we assume it does occur, doesn't count.

It is perhaps also because society in general, and women in particular, have more to fear from psychic disorders in men, since the effects can be devastating.[26] Phyllis Chesler[27] pointed out how quickly women showing signs of 'unfeminine behaviour' get psychiatric treatment and are thereby rendered socially innocuous and harmless. Unlike men. Has experience and a deep-seated fear of the tyranny of wrongly channelled manliness made women infinitely more sensitive towards their sons than their daughters?

13 January 1984 (2 years 5 months)
We're invited to Jürgen's house in the evening. He tells Anneli that he had peas and carrots (a favourite of hers) at lunchtime; she has to guess who cooked them. He makes the tale really exciting, so of course she has no idea. Then he announces splendidly that he cooked them *himself*, because his wife Ulla wasn't at home. Anneli listens attentively and with understanding, and although she says nothing I can see from her face that she has taken it all in. And what sticks in her mind is that it is quite exceptional and really special when the husband does the cooking, that he only does it when the wife's away. But then of course it's worth talking about

and the meal is also particularly good, as the link with favourite food indicates. Even here – if he has to cook – he does it better. This seems to be a principle that has permeated many cultures. In Berlin in 1984 and in Bali in 1930. Margaret Mead writes of Bali: 'One aspect of the social valuation of different types of labour is the different prestige of men's activities and women's activities. Whatever men do – even if it is dressing dolls for religious ceremonies – is more prestigious that what women do and is treated as a higher achievement.'[28]

14 January 1984 (2 years 5 months)

Uschi and her daughter, Annalena, (ten months old) are visiting us. Uschi and I are sitting over a cup of tea, knitting and chatting; our topic is the usual one: children, how and when they eat, sleep, pee and get on our nerves.

So that we can talk undisturbed I tell Anneli to play with Annalena; the bigger girl is told to play with the smaller one so Mum can have a rest. Would I have done that quite so automatically with a boy?

Uschi is telling me about her analysis, father complex, etc., and in some connection the phrase 'only a girl' crops up. At that moment Anneli, who is sitting next to us, stops playing with her doll, lifts her head and looks at me questioningly. But she doesn't say anything and soon goes on playing.

15 January 1984 (2 years 5 months)

Whilst we're having breakfast Anneli says to me, 'Now I'm the Mummy and you're my friend and now we're talking, this is my baby and when it eats it goes like this [she makes suitable movements with hand and arm] and then it goes to bed.' She uses the exact intonation adopted by Uschi and me when we had been gossiping the day before. She has understood perfectly what women who have children talk about when they're together.

In the afternoon we go and see Sabine, and Ursel joins us for tea. So there are three women sitting round the kitchen table, all knitting. Anneli stands on the bench and announces clearly, 'Everybody's knitting.' Then she wanders into the other room and sees the two men who live there with papers or books and comes back and says, 'The men are reading, Mummy.'

I can't tell whether these pronouncements are linked with any gender categories. Anneli has seen a lot of women knitting, but not a single man. If the total picture of what women and men do is made up of many individual experiences then women and knitting certainly go together.

16 January 1984 (2 years 5 months)

We're at Angela's. Anneli looks at herself in Angela's concave mirror and announces, 'Now I'm big, now I'm a boy.' Big is still a synonym for being able and allowed to do things. Angela and I are horrified, but speechless. Angela is the first to find her tongue, and she says, 'No, boys are little and silly.'

Where on earth did Anneli get this idea? Was it the conversation with Uschi – 'only a girl'? Or have we once again to say that it's simply part of the environment? Is Angela's unambiguous answer the right one, because by responding to the deceits of our society in which men appear to children to be bigger and better with an equally radical lie untruths are balanced, or it is wrong to say this because it does not correspond to social reality? We just hope and believe that our interpretation of things might provide a counter balance in the child's mind.

17 January 1984 (2 years 5 months)

In the morning we're lying in bed playing 'baby in tummy' and 'baby is born.' As usual she curls herself up on my tummy, then crawls down and creeps out from under the quilt at the bottom of the bed. Then she goes through the same game with her toy cat. It lies on her tummy, is then pushed down and Anneli says 'It's born.' I lay the little cat on her chest and say that now it's drinking like babies at their mother's breast. She squeaks with pleasure and repeats my action again and again.

I'm sure this game would never have occurred to me with a boy. This sort of preparation for the sexual role can only be passed on to girls. At this early stage the harmony of person, identity and sex occurs only in girls. It is possible to show her that later she'll have a baby, just as she once was, but such sexual identity cannot be passed on to a boy. Margaret Mead said that girls very early became aware of their future maternal role, which needed no further justification through personal achievements.[29] In Mead it's the life of the tribe that gives girls this awareness; with us it's mothers' stories and their games.

18 January 1984 (2 years 5 months)
Anneli stops in front of an antiquarian bookshop window, in which there's a display about old railways. She looks at them carefully and then says, 'Daddy always stops here to have a look.' Suddenly she's very keen on railways. I stand in front of the shop feeling bored, because I really wanted to buy her some trousers. I'm on the point of tempting her to move on, as I'm not interested in trains, when I remember how often I have previously been surprised by her lack of interest in trains. I was ready to admit that this was because girls aren't interested in technical things.

Realising this, I stay with her and *together* – in contrast to earlier occasions – we talk about trains and all the things we see in the window. She wants to play with them. Normally by now at the very latest I would have had enough, and would have told her that we didn't have enough time as we had to go shopping; that would have been that, despite any protests she might have made. But now I'm very aware of what's going on so I try to think of a way out. Then I remember a toy shop not far away where there are usually some model railways on display. I take her there and we don't miss anything important; and the shopping can be put off for an hour. I do all this quite consciously so as not to fail yet again to acknowledge her keen interest in something simply because it's unimportant to *me*; so I spend some time making an effort to show interest in all the equipment, the engines and little lamps. I'm sure that I would have brought a son to this shop long ago. Right from the start I would have assumed that he had different interests from me and would have been awake to things that might interest him when I went out. Never would I have dreamt of pulling him away from railway displays he found interesting. I wonder how often I've done that to Anneli?

In the afternoon she gives a friend a detailed description of her new bed in Munich. 'Daddy put a screw in there, and then he did like this and this and then there's a rail, so I don't fall out.' And she moves her arms and mimes Klaus putting the bed together. This was all two months ago. Daddy did build the bed, of course, though I paid no attention at the time. But Anneli draws my attention long afterwards to the impression she has gained of things. Once again I had been unaware of this at the time – or I might have got hold of some tools myself. How on earth is my daughter supposed to pick up tools quite naturally if I never set her an example?

20 January 1984 (2 years 5 months)
Back in Munich we're unpacking, and Grandma is here. The little screwdriver I bought Anneli falls out of her toy box and Grandma says, 'So you took Daddy's screwdriver with you?'

I suppose it's obvious that if there's no other man in the house then the screwdriver must belong to Daddy. I bet if she'd been talking to a grandson Grandma would have said, 'So you took your screwdriver with you, what did you mend in Berlin then?' But with a girl the screwdriver has to be Daddy's as there's no question of it being her own. I reply quickly, 'No, it's hers.' Anneli herself says nothing, though she's usually very precise about what belongs to her. I don't know whether she registers my comment at all.

21 January 1984 (2 years 5 months)
Anneli, her best friend Schorschi and I have been invited to coffee this afternoon at Hannelore's. Our hostess is 35, a nursery nurse, with a keen political awareness and a generally critical approach to life. She wants her two sons (4 and 10 years old) to be different and is convinced she's not bringing them up to be Men.

We're sitting at the table talking and the children, plus some other little friends of the younger son, are playing with some Duplo and Lego parts. It's very peaceful. Hannelore starts to say how nice it would have been to have had instead of two sons a girl as well as a boy. 'Little girls are so sweet.' And she bends over to Anneli, interrupts her, picks her up and gives her a cuddle. Anneli looks in wonder from Hannelore to the building sets. Then Hannelore really gets going. 'Aren't you a little sweetie with your lovely curls?' Her voice has become a high singsong. 'Can you do your hair yourself?'

Anneli manages a well behaved 'yes' – although it's not true; she knows what's expected of her and she goes on, 'I've got a mirror and I go like this and like this,' and she runs her fingers through her hair – her way of doing it. Hannelore is delighted and then asks Anneli whether she does her dolls' hair, what they're called and whether they're big or small. Then she says again what a sweetie Anneli is.

In the meantime the boys have continued to play uninterrupted.

Hannelore releases Anneli, putting her back down on the floor. But now there are problems with the boys; they no longer want Anneli to take any of the pieces and start squabbling. To avoid too much fuss Hannelore picks Anneli up again, saying 'Come on, Poppet.' And there she stays, withdrawn from the boys' game, being fed with little pieces of chocolate cake from Hannelore's plate.

The boys stuff cake into their mouths and continue playing on the floor.

The whole gathering is then moved into the living room, where there's plenty of space. A squabble starts. Hannelore again gets hold of Anneli, saying, 'Come on darling, leave the silly boys to their squabbles.'

When we leave Anneli is overwhelmed with kisses; Schorschi gets a pat on the shoulder and a jolly 'Cheerio.'

22 January 1984 (2 years 5 months)

I'm out with Schorschi and Anneli delivering invitations to a meeting. Ingrid's door opens; she is a teacher with a progressive approach to education. Anneli and Schorschi are in front of me. In their snowsuits, with their bright blue eyes and brilliant smiles, they do make a lovely picture. Ingrid says hello and we talk briefly. Then she turns to the children. 'Well, Schorschi, it's lovely to see you; have you been busy tobogganing?' She speaks in a normal, cheerful tone, the pitch unchanged. Then she bends over Anneli, gives her a brilliant smile, puts her arm round her, picks her up and says, 'Hello, Poppet, don't you look pretty today? And what lovely curls; they are growing quickly. I've got something for you.' Her vocal pitch has risen noticeably and the final words are spoken in a particularly ingratiating tone. Schorschi is still standing there, looking up at Ingrid with Anneli in her arms. Then Ingrid disappears into the house with Anneli and fetches a pretzel. She wants a kiss from Anneli in exchange, and then she begins to tickle and tease her and admires her hat and her snowsuit, which are all quite normal articles of clothing. Schorschi has been standing alongside all the time but now he trots off and plays in the snow, leaving Anneli tight in Ingrid's arms.

Is it surprising that girls can relate to people better and boys are so neutral?

24 January 1984 (2 years 5 months)

We're off to Switzerland for a winter holiday and since it's snowing heavily have to put snow chains on the car. Klaus makes a start and I join in. Anneli sits on her toboggan whingeing and complaining because she's bored. Klaus wants me to play with her because her whining gets on his nerves while he's doing this. Of course, I'm the one who's supposed to play with her while he messes around with the car, although I'm perfectly capable of mounting chains. So I stay put, let her whinge and tell her that Mummy and Daddy are putting chains on the car wheels so that we can use the car. Without my constant reference to this diary I wouldn't have done that – I'd have done as I was told. And Klaus of all people, who often complains that I don't concern myself enough with technical things, is taking a very conservative line now: forget the car, woman; take care of the child.

When we're under pressure we revert to our traditional roles.

27 January 1984 (2 years 5 months)

On my walks through the village with Anneli I often meet other women with small children. The children are all well wrapped up in their snowsuits and with the best will in the world you can't tell which sex they are. In casual conversations with women I notice that after the first few sentences we quickly ask whether the child is a boy or a girl. I ask just like everyone else; it's pure chance whether I or my conversation partner is the first to ask.

Have I now fallen victim to prejudice, able after the 'decisive' question has been answered to judge a boy's vitality, aggressiveness and robustness, to compare him with Anneli – or not, because I expect different qualities in boys? I catch myself thinking and noticing such things.

1 Feburary 1984 (2 years 6 months)

I think about the *lederhose* I bought for Anneli at a Berlin flea market. When I bought them I fancied the image of the cheeky little urchin I thought Anneli would look in leather shorts, and it seemed a good idea then for her clothes to be practical rather than feminine. On the other hand, a girl in *lederhose* is particularly 'cute'. Is it for this reason that I want her to wear them? I think I've caught myself out again.

But then I project the problem into the future. The shorts are so big that they won't fit Anneli for a few years yet, anyway, and I wonder whether she'll want to wear them by then. A girl! What would her friends at playgroup say about them? Am I making an outsider of her? Now I'm automatically assuming that by the time she's five or six Anneli will identify so strongly as a girl that she won't want to wear the shorts. But I'm aware that this is my projection of her behaviour as a girl. I am taking for granted I know what will by then be socially acceptable for a girl, even if this is only within the social framework of playgroup.

So then I offer Christa the *lederhose* for Schorschi. To which she responds by enquiring whether they're really a boy's pair, that is, 'proper' *lederhose*.

We're really outdoing one another here with our hang-ups, aren't we? And so we make women and men of our children with our attitudes and different tastes.

2 February 1984 (2 years 6 months)

Grandma's visiting us. Anneli disturbs her as she's making the breakfast and I hear Grandma trying to find something for her to do. 'Go and see if Sleepy Head [one of the Christmas dolls] needs changing, whether her nappy's dirty.' This is how a girl's persuaded to play with dolls.

When we're out shopping we meet Barbara with Felix. Barbara explains that she's on her way to the clinic to ask whether Felix is old enough to have a pedal car – because he likes cars so much. I'd never thought of getting Anneli a pedal car; is that once again because I'm not interested in cars?

3 February 1984 (2 years 6 months)

We are drawing and Anneli wants to do a picture of the Holy Family in Egypt, Joseph as a carpenter with hammer and nails, the Christ Child in the crib with Mary beside him. I draw Joseph with a pipe hanging from the side of his mouth, just like the old hunter we saw in Switzerland. Anneli wants Mary to have a pipe, too, and I say without thinking, 'But Mary can't smoke a pipe.' Whereupon Anneli responds, 'But women can smoke pipes – they taste good.' (The old Swiss hunter had told her that.) So now I add, 'Of course women can smoke pipes.'

At the same time I think of two women colleagues of mine who both smoke cigars and who both meet rudeness from male colleagues and disdain from women. I find this behaviour very intolerant, but now I catch myself doing more or less the same thing. Do I correct myself only because I have the continual check of this diary? Would I otherwise have insisted that Mary couldn't have a pipe? I'm not sure.

In the afternoon she's playing with two little boys (two and three years old) in her room. The three of them come out each with a wooden spill in their mouths. Anneli says, 'These are our cigarettes and we're smoking.' I respond, 'That's not a very nice toy.' She's outraged, 'But I'm a man!'

Is this morning's lesson already having its effect? The boys' mothers let them keep their 'cigarettes', even though they agree with me that it's not a good game, simply because it encourages smoking.

During her evening bath she stands up in the tub, places her hands in front of her and says she's having a pee. She's trying to imitate men. Grandma says, 'Stop that, you're a girl, not a boy.' Again the rule of behaviour that determines what women and girls may and may not do. Certainly not what boys do.

4 February 1984 (2 years 6 months)
Anneli and I are looking at a picture book about Egyptian mythology which happens to be in the room and in which she shows interest. She looks at a very stylised male deity and says, 'Who's that?' I reply, 'That's a sort of guru.' She knows what that is because we once visited a friend's ashram.

Anneli then asks, 'Is it a man?' and I reply, quite spontaneously, 'No, it's a woman.'

In an attempt to re-establish equilibrium, at least in heaven, I lie, because I'm sick of having to leave these constellations to men. Only later, after I've been having scruples about it, do I tell myself that it's not really a lie, anyway. There were once matriarchies, or at least transitional periods, when goddesses ruled alone, or at least had dominant positions.[30]

Despite all this I saw my representation of a god as female as a lie, and I'm appalled at how deeply rooted the primacy of the male god is and how we withhold from our daughters the real, hard-won knowledge of female history. I reacted as I did, not from my knowledge of goddesses, but from sheer stubbornness and with a bad conscience.

6 February 1984 (2 years 6 months)
At breakfast today Anneli talks about making a mess with food on the table and mentions that Felix does this. When I explain that Felix is smaller than she is, almost still a baby really (two months younger in fact) and that that's why he can't eat properly yet, she says, 'But Felix is bigger than me, and Schorschi [one month younger] is as well.'

I say, 'No, they're both smaller than you,' to which she replies, 'No, they're boys and boys are bigger than me.'

I'm shocked by this statement, since to Anneli being bigger means being able to do things and allowed to do them. I ask her who told her this. She says it was Barbara, Felix's mother. I don't believe this and can only imagine that she had misunderstood one mother saying to another that boys were bigger in size and interpreted this in terms of her expectations of life. Another of those ominous 'atmospheric' items that help give boys an advantage, and teach girls to respect the male and give them that insidious, lifelong inferiority complex. Anneli has picked quite a bit of this up, as one can see from her comments.

In the afternoon she's sitting in the lavatory chattering to herself. She says, 'Schorschi is a boy and I'm a girl.'

I ask, 'What's Daddy?'

She: 'A boy.'

I: 'And what's Mummy?'

She: 'A boy.' I laugh.

When she comes back into the living room she says, 'Everybody's a boy, I'm the only girl.' She seems to have internalised a hierarchy in which the person on the bottom rung has to be a girl; all the others are boys.

In the afternoon she paints a breast on her doll and in the evening she wants to paint breasts on Klaus's chest. Breasts are terribly important.

Outside she's hammering nails into the wall with her little wooden mallet. She really enjoys it and I encourage her. Then she says with some satisfaction, 'Just like Daddy.' I feel peeved because she's seen me knock in enough nails. But it can't have been enough, or wasn't demonstrative enough.

10 February 1984 (2 years 6 months)
In the morning Schorschi and Anneli are playing with baby dolls. Anneli holds the doll in her arms, rocks it and sings it a song. She's standing at the door to the veranda, holding the 'baby' in the sun. She makes a touching picture and is standing in just the position I used to hold her in. For a moment I feel quite overwhelmed.

I spend the afternoon and evening away from Anneli and when I get home and we're having supper I want to be especially loving towards her. Suddenly I get the idea of giving her my old little tortoiseshell doll to play with, one which is very like the doll she had this morning. At the same time I do realise that I had intended not to encourage playing with dolls as Grandma does more than enough in this respect. But I can't resist and give her the doll. She's in raptures with it and we play with it together.

Isn't this the typical girls' upbringing, so often referred to in studies and statistics? This morning Schorschi was also playing with his dolls, but no one gave him an extra one as *his* baby and then played with it with him.

11 February 1984 (2 years 6 months)
Anneli and I go to an exhibition of children's books. The librarian comes over to us and recommends books by Janosch as being particularly nice. I don't react to this since I consider these books to be sexist, but I don't tell her that. I look at the books on display.

My attention is particularly drawn to two books on careers, which exceed all the others in veiled discrimination. One of them has a frontispiece showing a large house, open at the front so children can see into the various rooms. And what can they see there? There are *eight* different men in typically masculine jobs. Women appear as a patient at the doctor's, a witness with a judge, a schoolgirl with a teacher. The book is in my opinion a complete misrepresentation of social reality. So why do I need to have any scruples when I include women, as with the orchestra or the gods, for example? This book simply denies the existence of the numerous women doctors, judges, lawyers, teachers, engineers and architects. I get quite furious and decide I'm going to get my own back by talking about professions in future as being the prerogative of women. The second book depicts only men, this time in blue-collar jobs such as dredger drivers, plumbers, bakers, cooks and house painters.

I'm so annoyed that I actually say so to the librarian. She reacts quite sympathetically, agrees with what I say and it becomes clear that she also thinks that Janosch is sexist. This quite takes my breath away. Why did she recommend him to me before she knew what my opinions were? Is it because I'm not dressed obviously like a feminist? Are these opinions only to be shared with insiders? I don't quite know what to make of this sudden change of attitude. I ask her whether she thinks that girls' mothers borrow different books from boys' mothers. She says they do. Girls get books about horses and other animals, mystery books and fairy tales, whereas boys get adventure stories, travel and career books. From the age of seven, she assures me, the difference in lending happens automatically. No doubt that's due to the oft quoted instinct that makes boys different from girls?

Moreover, over lunch, the librarian, who has a four-year-old son, assures me that boys really are different from girls – even when they're brought up the same. She didn't want her boy to become a Real Man, but he is turning out to be a typical boy. There must be an innate difference, she says she now has to admit, although she had previously not believed this.

12 February 1984 (2 years 6 months)

Anneli's snowman, which we built yesterday, has been destroyed. She cries her eyes out. Without thinking, I tell her some stupid boys must have done it, quite spontaneously ascribing force, aggression and destruction to masculine beings. Probably because my experience of life has shown me this is so and thus to me it is a social reality. (Boxing, rape, the military, war, criminality, a whole range of violent situations occur to me which are the domain of men.)

Anneli might, of course, infer from this that such deeds are acceptable for the boys who commit them but not for girls. Her attempt to find comfort in the threat 'We'll hit them' is immediately followed by the realisation that 'They'll hit us back', and her sobbing increases at the awareness of her own impotence. This confirms my impression that she is unable to conceive of any reaction to physical violence, which she has only ever experienced from boys, that might possibly prevent it; that hitting is only reciprocated with more hitting and does not solve the conflict is something she has already learned from experience. She doesn't hit back, rejecting the masculine principle of an eye for an eye and a tooth for a tooth and realising that such a principle must go on *ad absurdum*. But why does she have this feeling of impotence? Because we haven't found an answer; because we mothers are unable to offer anything but patriarchal possibilities for solving conflict; because violence isn't 'atmospherically' branded and outlawed – except, of course, for women and girls.

In the kitchen in the afternoon Schorschi is waving a cloth right in front of Anneli's face, assuming a threatening pose and shouting at her. He's only having fun but she feels intimidated and threatened. She puts her head down, holds her arm up to protect herself and screams. Perhaps she's still too affected by the loss of her snowman to understand a joke. I go over to her, give her a cloth as well and wave it in front of Schorschi's face; now she understands and quietens down. But she doesn't like threatening games, and Schorschi is in no way intimidated by her. Once again a boy has the 'atmosphere' in his favour and the girl had to react, to understand what to do. Neither of us mothers stops Schorschi because he is frightening Anneli, though his behaviour is an expression of violence. Anneli must assume he's allowed to do that, it's just the way things are. It's not surprising that girls, and later women, have such feelings of impotence when we are never shown any other ways of behaving – and this particular behaviour is in any case socially unacceptable and not expected from us. Here already a girl begins to suffer the consequences of the contradiction between behaviour that would be practical and behaviour that society expects of her.

13 February 1984 (2 years 6 months)
I have to take something to Christa's. She has visitors and we have a cup of coffee together. Inevitably we start talking about children: how tall, how fat, how clever, how jolly. Anneli and Schorschi are discussed in detail and at length. Christa's brother-in-law says, 'Schorschi has very delicate features, almost like a girl. It bodes no good for his future for him to be soft and perhaps mistaken for a girl.' What image is he projecting on to this two-and-a-half-year-old? Is it surprising that people who say things like this treat children differently according to their sex and interpret their behaviour in different ways?

14 February 1984 (2 years 6 months)
We're in town in the afternoon and, despite the hat that boys' mothers have described as feminine, several people address Anneli as a boy. When I think about it I suddenly see the connection between this and the way we use language.

People assume in our society that the object of their attention is a man, just as language defines everything initially as masculine.[31] As, for example, in the concept 'man', which can include women as well. The tone is set by the masculine, which is definitive. Therefore people assume that a child which is dressed fairly neutrally is a boy. Only when they're corrected by the child or a chilly smile from the mother do they politely enquire whether the child might after all be a girl. It goes like this, 'So you're a little girl then, are you?' The divergence from what had been assumed has first to be made clear to strangers. The girls must get the impression that being a girl is something odd, something they weren't expecting, a divergence from the norm.

15 February 1984 (2 years 6 months)
We're in Munich and look at books on display in a bookshop. On the bottom shelf, at children's eye level, some children's books are set out, three next to one another with the titles, *I am the Doctor, I am the Fisherman, I am the Cook*. The covers show pictures of boys, with self-confident smiles, wearing the professional garb of doctor, fisherman and cook. There are no girls at all in the pictures. Anneli looks at them and then asks what those boys are doing. Annoyed once again by the sexism I don't tell Anneli

they're jobs but simply say the boys are playing games we could also play at home.

Is falsifying reality like this the only way of keeping *all* professions open to my daughter? I wonder whether Anneli knows any women doctors or whether she has encountered any women in this profession at all. No, for the pediatrician we went to for all the usual checks and tests was a man; my dentist, whom she has been to with me, is a man; the doctor we saw in Berlin was also a man. I resolve that the next time we have to go to the doctor I shall quite definitely choose a woman, so that Anneli has this possibility of identification.

Two weeks later her ear is inflamed and I decide we'll see a woman homeopathist. When Anneli is better, she plays at hospital and being sick with three-year-old Hanna, talking all the time about the woman doctor. From now on I do my remedial gymnastics with a woman, as a counter balance to what had gone before.

Another lie?

16 February 1984 (2 years 6 months)

Anneli comes back from the babysitter's with bright red fingernails again. The first thing she says is, 'It's because I'm a lady.' Schorschi is with her, but his nails have not been varnished. I admire her, with a certain amount of reserve, and ask Tini why Schorschi hasn't got any nail varnish on.

Anneli butts in without letting Tini speak: 'Schorschi's a man, not a lady. I'm a lady.' Then she holds out her fingers again to show me. I can well imagine what sort of tale Tini has been telling them.

18 February 1984 (2 years 6 months)

We're spending a week on a farm in the South Tyrol. There are three girls in the family: Bernadette, who is four, Anna, like Anneli going on for three, and Magdalena, one year old.

For a week the three older girls play with one another without any problems of pushing or fighting. Of course, they quarrel from time to time about some toy or other, but otherwise there are no problems. There is none of the aggression I'm used to with boys.

Anneli and Anna are having a joke. They nudge one another, giggling as they do so. They test the effect of the nudging by slowly increasing the force. Each of them measures her strength exactly and is very gentle with the other, until they both fall down and roll on the floor, on top and underneath one another, back and forth, cuddling more than wrestling and both finding pleasure in the contact, without any trace of aggression or ambition to fight. It reminds me of women's conversations as described by linguists such as Senta Trömel-Plötz.[32]

Later on I'm talking with Anna's mother, Frau Gärtner, about problems of aggression. She tells me how Anna once gave a smaller child such a prod that it fell down, how she scolded Anna and probably smacked her, and that it's never happened again. I remember that I reacted pretty energetically to Anneli's first efforts in this direction. Clearly we've checked aggression in our daughters at a very early stage.

The children are having great fun playing with Anneli's little work bench. Frau Gärtner thinks it's a lovely toy and that it would be especially good for a boy.

We talk about her fourth child and how she hopes it will be a boy. Frau Gärtner says she doesn't know how to bring up a boy; she'll have to learn, since so far she has only reared girls. In a simple, conservative manner she makes it clear that there are two ways of bringing up children, according to whether they're girls or boys.

22 February 1984 (2 years 6 months)

We're buying shoes for Anneli in Bolzano, in northern Italy, and I find a really sensible pair, brown and without any fashionable frills. The South Tyrolean farmers buy shoes here, as the style suggests. But at first I feel that the shoes aren't quite right. I ask to see other models, but there aren't any more. Only then does it occur to me that the reason why I'm reluctant to buy these shoes, which are just right, is because they look to me like boys' shoes – because there's nothing on them to indicate that they're for girls. But what's that supposed to mean? What is it that makes a shoe a girl's shoe? I see how silly this is and buy the shoes, which Anneli likes and which seem really sensible. If I hadn't thought carefully about this I would have continued in search of 'girls'' shoes. Well, taste and the need for decoration must come from somewhere.

I'm sitting with the three girls in a café when Anneli suddenly asks if Anna and Bernadette also have breasts. I say 'Yes,' and that's that.

Frau Gärtner tells us that when Anna and Bernadette first saw a little boy without any clothes on, they thought he was ill because he had a terrible little tail dangling between his legs. They called for their Mummy to help him. I'm pleased to find evidence in the girls' behaviour of what Kate Millett and Simone de Beauvoir suggest when discussing the Freudian theory of penis envy.[33] Both ask why girls should be immediately convinced that the bigger (penis compared to clitoris) is also better. Isn't a child just as likely, from simple childish narcissism, to assume that a penis is a growth and take her own body as the norm?

In the meantime the existence of breasts plays a much larger role in Anneli's preoccupations than a penis. She points to her own breast and judges people according to having and not having. Schorschi also joins in the conversations about breasts enthusiastically and with great interest.

But so far I've never heard a murmur about boys and men having a breast complex.

2 March 1984 (2 years 7 months)

Klaus and Anneli are both ill and in bed. She decides that his beard scratches. She thinks when she grows up she'll have a beard. Klaus says she won't and explains that girls and women don't have beards and that she'll be like Mummy. So now she insists that when Mummy grows bigger she'll have a beard as well.

I hear these discussions from the living room and realise that in the world of her ideas I am obviously not as big as Daddy but occupy a space somewhere between child and Daddy; where there's any doubt, though, I belong to the category of children, for I can still grow to be as big as Daddy and approach his perfection.

3 March 1984 (2 years 7 months)

Today I played a game of slapping and tussling with Anneli. I avoid doing anything more than just tapping her, but when I do give her a hard tap she's frightened and asks why I'm angry. I remember the problems I had with ju-jitsu classes in dealing with aggression at close quarters, in approaching a person with the intention of striking them in the face with my fist. At the start I found I couldn't do it and only training made it possible. But that was all a long time ago – I'm still the person I used to be, unable to attack anyone else.

I behave the same way to Anneli, not really trying to get hold of her, for she's just a girl like me. From my point of view she doesn't need the 'other'. Is it the same as with the cars and machines? Does the fact that we are the same prevent me from imagining it could be different? Is this how the sameness, that is, 'femininity', is handed on?

In the evening I am briefly at Christa's. Though it's ten o'clock for some reason Schorschi can't sleep and Christa gets him out of bed. He gives me a very unfriendly look. I accept this quite simply as masculine lack of interest or even frank rejection, like the attitude of grown men, and I don't make any attempt to persuade him to smile or be 'nice'. In the case of a little girl I think I would have acted more emotionally; I would have made a real effort to tempt a smile out of her. I'm sure I wouldn't have left her in the mood she was in but would have tried to change it – to one that suited me better. The boy is accepted as he is, but girls are tempted or encouraged, perhaps forcefully, to other, more friendly, attitudes. Is it any wonder that we run round like smiling machines?

4 March 1984 (2 years 7 months)

We have been invited to Friedrich's second birthday party. There's another boy there who is almost four and he goes straight up to Anneli, holds up his arm, bends it and says, 'Look at my muscles.' As he does so it seems to me that there's an undertone of threat and masculine superiority in his manner. Without waiting for Anneli's reaction I butt in, telling him that Anneli also has big muscles, and at my instigation Anneli also demonstrates her 'biceps'. The boy leaves us without another word. Anneli says, 'I've got big muscles, haven't I, Mummy?' and I tell her she has. The boy turns to another girl with the same approach. She gazes at him in wonderment and says nothing. Then her mother and another guest go up to them and now the two grown women stand there admiring the physique of this four-year-old, whose muscles are no different at all from those of the girl standing next to him. The world's in order as far as the boy's concerned and the girls have learned a lesson. A couple of minutes later our hostess comes into the room

asking for a 'strong man' to give her a hand fixing a curtain rail
that has fallen down. This has got nothing to do with strength but
with work. I wonder what use my little pedagogic effort on
muscles is when it's immediately followed by this crass example,
and strength is proclaimed loud and clear by several women to be
an attribute of men, large and small.

One of the boys takes a little figure made of sugar away from
Anneli, which our hostess had just given her. Anneli yells and
wants to grab it back off him; she almost succeeds but he's too
quick and sticks it in his mouth. Anneli screams with rage. The
boys' parents are standing next to the children, watching; they tell
Anneli to be a bit more careful and a bit quicker next time. Not a
word to the boy who has snatched the thing from her, no admoni-
tion to him not to do it again. Once again it's the girl who is told to
alter her behaviour. Even in cases where the boy has used force
and is in the wrong the girl is expected to prevent this happening
again by adapting her behaviour. To me it's the same as in rape
trials, where the woman is always in the wrong. *She* should have
realised early enough what his intentions were and changed her
behaviour accordingly. *He* can do what he likes; it's always the
girls who have to adapt.

As we are leaving I notice how the other women modify their
voices when taking leave of boys and girls. With boys the tone is
firm, loud, cheerful and brisk, accompanied by a handshake or a
slap on the shoulders; they speak to the girls in high, gentle voices,
saying in mild tones, 'Bye bye, lovey' or 'Cheerio, poppet' or 'Ta
ta, you little sweetie pie'.

5 March 1984 (2 years 7 months)

We're visiting a family where there are two boys. The whole room
is full of Duplo pieces with cranes and dredgers, and Anneli wants
to play with them. Although there are plenty of them lying around,
Sebastian (who is four) wants just those pieces Anneli has and tries
to take them off her. She resists but she doesn't get far because
Sebastian is bigger and stronger. We mothers look on. Only when
Sebastian has won does his mother intervene to give Anneli back
the pieces. But the negotiations between mother and son take some
time and by the time they've finished Anneli has lost interest.
When the Duplo pieces are given to her she doesn't want them

any more but now devotes herself to a little wicker pram with dolls in it, the only toys there apart from the Duplo set. Now she starts to play mother and baby and Sebastian's mother remarks that she can play with them in peace because Sebastian isn't interested. Which is true enough.

Once again it was the girl who had to find something the boy wasn't interested in; once again the boy was able to enjoy his dominance. Is it surprising she's not really interested in Duplo sets any more, but in what was left over for her? A reflection of our reality. We learn early on to be satisfied with our lot.

Some time later I see a very nice little wicker pram, similar to Sebastian's, at the market. I'm going to buy her it, but then I decide against it, to avoid adding yet another piece to the pattern: first she wants to build things; then she's prevented; then she plays nicely with the dolls; and finally she's rewarded with gifts to suit the doll game.

In the evening we discover her xylophone is broken. So who automatically sits down and repairs it? Klaus, of course. And I say, equally automatically, 'Look at Daddy mending your xylophone.'

6 March 1984 (2 years 7 months)

I often play a little music with Anneli on the piano, the recorder, the guitar or her tambourine. She sings nicely and after a few attempts manages all the notes of a children's song she knows. I think, or imagine, that she's musically gifted. All mothers at some point think their child might be a genius. I'm no different and I fantasise about the great things she might achieve in music. Names occur to me: Menuhin, Stern, Barenboim, Gould, Karajan, Furtwängler, Orff. All of them men – not a single woman's name occurs to me, although I'm perfectly aware there are some very talented women musicians. They're famous, too, but they're not geniuses! To my horror I find myself ready instinctively to abandon my wild dreams of great musical genius, because she's a girl. In a fraction of a second the idea flashes through my mind, 'She's a woman, so she won't be a great genius but she might develop a nice little talent.'

What effect might such an attitude have? Am I likely to give up, believing it's not worth investing effort in an unattainable goal?

How many girls who really were born to genius has this happened to in the course of history? Perhaps it's not only the conscious falsification of history that has left us so few female geniuses, but the fact that lack of faith deterred young girls from the very start. The genius in the Mozart family might otherwise have been called Amanda rather than Amadeus.

7 March 1984 (2 years 7 months)
Anneli and I are out in central Munich and we pass the same bookshop we had looked into three weeks ago (15 February). More books about careers are on display: *I am the Little Nurse*, *I am the Dancer*, *I am the Farmer's Wife*, all with pictures of little girls suitably attired. I drag Anneli past as quickly as I can.

8 March 1984 (2 years 7 months)
Schorschi hurt himself badly while he was out playing and has a cut in his head that has to be stitched. We go to the doctor's. Schorschi is already lying on the table when the doctor comes into the room. He speaks to Schorschi very mildly, touches him gently, addresses him as a girl and asks what he's called. Then it comes out that Schorschi's a boy. The doctor apologises profusely for his mistake and immediately adopts a more robust tone; from now on he talks as though from man to man. He stresses that Schorschi will have to be brave, says it doesn't matter if he cries because it's going to hurt so much. He's particularly nice to Schorschi now, giving the impression that he's very embarrassed at having mistaken Schorschi for a girl and wanting to make up for his blunder. And all this in front of a girl, for Anneli is with us. No one says anything to her and I wonder how much of it she understands.

In the evening she says to me, 'When I'm big, Mummy, I'll be able to have a baby, won't I?' My 'yes' appears to satisfy her. For some weeks she has been putting her doll on her tummy at bedtime. She obviously likes playing at being pregnant and is fully aware of her sexual identity. She then plays at breast feeding and lays the doll on her chest.

9 March 1984 (2 years 7 months)
Sophie, a friend of mine, is visiting us. Maybe *Fasching** has got

* The pre-lenten carnival period. (*Translator's note.*)

into us, but anyway Sophie and I are tussling on the floor over one of Anneli's dolls. Anneli watches us rolling on the floor in amazement. After a while I've had enough and want to stop. But Sophie is really getting into the spirit of the thing and I feel under some pressure to continue, to show Anneli that it's not only fathers and sons that go in for such rough and tumble.

What am I trying to prove? Is it because she's rather timid in the face of aggressive behaviour in the playground and I think our example might help her get over her inhibitions and that she might occasionally hit back? Why should she learn to hit back, anyway? Boys' mothers are always saying she should. When children are squabbling mothers are supposed not to interfere – 'the children have to sort it out themselves and after all girls must learn to stick up for themselves'. But how on earth can they learn this as easily as boys, who often wrestle with their fathers, when they never see women grappling or wrestling with one another? So I have to set her an example.

I think how clever I am. It doesn't occur to me that I'm only teaching her to copy masculine behaviour, to adapt yet again.

A bit later she takes my sunglasses from a drawer, puts them on, stands in front of me with her legs wide apart – as far as possible – and says, 'Now I'm a man as well.' I don't know what she means until I glance through these notes and find the entry of 16 September describing the incredible impression the bus driver in the Engadine made on her with his sunglasses. A truly masculine bus driver, of course.

I'm surprised at what little details of outer appearance children base their gender categorisation on.

14 March 1984 (2 years 7 months)
I'm in Berlin without Anneli. I have visitors: a 37-year-old woman with her son, Nik, who is five, and daughter, Hanna, who is three.

One morning I'm in my room and can hear Gisela, the mother, trying to persuade Hanna to let her plait her hair and fasten it with slides. Hanna is yelling and protesting energetically. For some time they get absolutely nowhere until Gisela says that Grandma likes her hair like that and since they're going to see Grandma now it would be really nice of Hanna to have her hair plaited like that, and what's more the slides she's got are really pretty ones. Hanna capitulates and lets her hair be plaited to please Grandma or her mother, albeit under protest. Nik, Hanna's brother, and his hair, are unmolested. He doesn't have to do anything or be nice to please people.

Sigmund Freud says of woman's need to decorate herself, 'The effect of penis-envy has a share, further, in the physical vanity of women, since they are bound to value their charms more highly as a late compensation for their original sexual inferiority.'[34]

Over breakfast we talk about what Gisela intends to do with the children in Berlin. She says, 'We want to go to the transport museum, to please Nik; he's bound to find that interesting and exciting and Hanna will have to go, too. There has to be something special for each of the children, so that they both enjoy themselves.'

Why does she assume that Hanna won't find the museum interesting as well? I'm convinced from what she says here that she'll devote less attention to Hanna when they're there than to Nik. Is this another example of what I've found to be true of myself, that is, mothers expect their daughters to be bored by what they themselves find uninteresting? When a girl has to join in activities undertaken principally for the sake of the male sibling that fact is emphasised well in advance. It's not surprising if the little girl feels bored.

Hanna comes into my room to show me a tiny baby doll. She explains, 'Mummy gave me this baby for the train journey, and knitted a jacket for it on the train, so it doesn't get cold.' And the doll really is dressed from head to foot in tiny knitted clothes. Now Nik joins us and proudly shows me what he got for the long train journey: a box of Lego and a car.

In the evening I talk with Gisela about the children, education, etc., and among other things ask her what gender specific tendencies she has noticed in the children. She starts by telling me that she doesn't make any distinction in the way she is bringing them up but that she has noticed quite marked natural differences: the girl's keen interest in dressing up, for example, and Nik's interest in technical things.

15 March 1984 (2 years 7 months)
My friend Angela and I are talking about an idea that Angela's boy friend might show Anneli his computer and let her play some

games on it, drawing pictures, etc. Later, Angela tells me how she has been studying computer technology and learning how to use one. We have been talking about this for some time before Angela announces with a huge smile that she will show Anneli the computer rather than her boy friend.

Why does it take two grown women, who think themselves emancipated, so long to notice that once again they are falling back on a man for help, assuming him to be competent instead of demonstrating the skills they themselves possess? Only by doing so themselves will new ideas ever be developed in children's minds. We women have to check and change ourselves and get down to business. Since knowledge of technology, which is dominated by men, is being continually renewed and extended, as the computer revolution shows, masculine hegemony continues. Further advances in technology have to be seen as an essential part of the historical development of the relationship between men and women and the values that are part of it. Only by participating can girls and women have any chance of influencing change, by persuading men in industry, for example, to see girls' potential and make more workplaces available.[35] But again who is expected to change? I long for an appeal to be made to small boys and men to reduce the speed of technological progress, by turning their energies and interest from technology towards the acquisition of human skills such as previously have only been attributed to women.

16 March 1984 (2 years 7 months)
At our mother and child gymnastics class in the afternoon Anneli manages a few rather nifty dance steps. Two boys are clumsily capering on the mat next to her trying in vain to imitate her. Comment from the boys' mothers: 'There again you see, boys are bigger [another general comment that boys are bigger in front of the children!] and stronger, but they are more wooden than the girls.'

Without thinking about this or questioning it at all the women attribute difference in performance to gender. So the problem's solved: anything girls can do and boys can't is simply due to gender difference. The boys stay just as they are and are not encouraged to imitate girls.

In fact, Anneli was able to do this because I've spent a lot of time dancing with her and we both enjoy it, and because she's learned some dancing at a music group. But I didn't say anything or encourage the boys to imitate her.

17 March 1984 (2 years 7 months)

I have bought a book that came out in the 1950s about Tom Thumb and we look at it together. The first picture shows a witch, represented as a wise woman giving a young woman a barley corn, which then turns into Tom Thumb. I'm relieved to find for the first time a positive representation of a witch in a children's book, as better fits historical truth and as I always try to teach Anneli. How rare texts and books of this sort are which give little girls a positive impression of old women and witches.

At breakfast Anneli's prattling on about destroying, about hitting, pulling people's ears and that it is boys who do this. I ask her what she means and once again hear the trauma of the destroyed snowman. Klaus had told her that on the day before he had seen two boys knocking the snowman down in front of our house. Now an image of rude and aggressive boys is firmly fixed in her mind. When I try to talk her out of it I am continually pulled up by the reality of Anneli's own experience of boys.

What are my powers of persuasion against her actual experience?

19 March 1984 (2 years 7 months)

We have been invited to the house of a friend who has a son called Frieder (four months younger than Anneli). It's the same old story. Frieder thumps and shoves Anneli and takes the things she wants to play with away from her. So he's the victor. Frieder's mother intervenes, saying, 'Frieder, be nice to Anneli, give her the toys and stop shoving her, she's a girl.' In the course of the next few hours she repeats this several times as the situation demands.

Once again I don't quite know what to make of this way of teaching a boy to be polite. I suspect that the real problem is being played down and it is not the behaviour of two equal people that is under discussion, rather that an appeal is being made to the magnanimity of the one to give in to the other. This is an act of good will in which the parameters of power are clearly marked. The stronger of the two is being asked to be polite: instead of a demand being made to him to behave normally, a favour is requested. He is learning to dispense charity. Over and over again I have heard mothers say that children should be allowed to work out their own little disputes, that the weaker ones should be encouraged to stick up for themselves and that in general vigour will solve the conflict and, for example, procure possession of the spade. But this rule is modified on the occasions when politeness is being taught. In these cases this children's law of the jungle is set aside and magnanimity on the part of the stronger is encouraged, regardless of which of the fighting cocks was initially in the right. Thus the physically stronger boy learns how to judge and make concessions; the girl learns to wait upon his decision, to accept and submit to it, whatever he may decide. The boy is not expected to acknowledge who was right in the beginning, to forget his greater strength, to recognise that two little human beings of equal value are confronting one another; no, he is expected to behave in a certain way because the other person is a girl. Mightn't a girl feel rather dismissed by all this? At least I can tell from Anneli's tense posture, from the uncertain expression on her face, from the imploring glances she gives me, that she is struggling with the injustice that has happened, between a desire to get her own way and capitulation in the face of the fact that an adult is letting the boy decide the problem. All she can do is wait or show her lack of interest in the object of the argument and withdraw from *his* sphere of competence.

I wonder whether I'm imagining all this, but then I find an article by psychologists interested in the subject.[36] They concluded that chivalry is a concealed or indirect form of misogyny which is only upheld in situations in which masculine dominance is in no doubt. A number of academic treatises are quoted which show that chivalrous behaviour towards women can be seen as part of a whole syndrome of conservative attitudes and behaviour. The authors conclude: 'In reality such forms of deference and consideration have more to do with the rules and rituals of etiquette than with any human concern for women. Chivalry has made a ritual of the physical superiority of the male. It is rarely available where there is any real need of assistance but only when magnanimous strength is not much use.'

So what is it our two-year-olds are learning when they are being taught good manners?

23 March 1984 (2 years 7 months)
Every day Anneli sees women looking after and caring for children. She neither sees men caring for babies to the same extent nor does she see the workplace of any of the men she knows. She has no idea what these men do, but is familiar enough with what women do, that is, feeding babies, changing nappies, teaching them to walk, loving them, etc.

I try to find a counter balance to this by reminding her of some women artist friends we visited and by talking expressly about women artists without mentioning men; by telling her that my workplace is a court of law and describing only women in it. I want her to link women with this sort of work, although it does contradict reality somewhat. Am I creating an artificial world for her?

In the afternoon Anneli, Schorschi and I visit an estate not far from us that is idyllically situated and which still has all the animals of an old style farm. We find a feather and I stick it in Anneli's hat – the girl's, of course, not the boy's – without thinking. She says, 'Now I'm a woman.' Again I'm surprised that Anneli defines women according to such trifling details, that for her sex is so dependent on appearance. In the South Tyrol, on the other hand, when looking at picture books Anna often defined people with feathers in their hats as Daddy. The national costume of the men in her village includes a hat with feathers in it.

24 March 1984 (2 years 7 months)
Schorschi and Anneli are at our house and having pancakes for lunch. I divide the portions on to two plates and notice that one is a bit bigger. Who do I give it to? Schorschi, of course, thinking that as a boy he is probably hungrier and will eat more than Anneli. I am transferring my expectations of masculine eating habits to a two-year-old boy. Having realised this I then pay attention and realise that Schorschi's portion is too much for him by just the extra amount I have given him and that he is no longer enjoying it. But at least I don't encourage him to eat it all up as I would probably otherwise have done, being of the opinion that I had given him the right amount.

Why do I think males always have to have more than females? Because my grandmother always gave the larger portion to Grandad and my mother to my father.

Technical point

25 March 1984 (2 years 7 months)
When Klaus comes home from work in the evening he brings Anneli two little toy cars and plays with them with her. When I interrupt them for some trifling matter, Klaus is annoyed and reproaches me for disturbing them just as he is explaining some technical point to Anneli. 'Explaining some technical point' does seem to be father's job and it occurs to me that recently it has always been me who has given Anneli dolls and Klaus who has given her construction toys and cars.

We discuss this later and decide that we both prefer the toys we ourselves had when young and are not interested in the toys of the opposite sex.

26 March 1984 (2 years 7 months)
The three of us are having breakfast. On the radio someone is playing a jew's harp. Klaus is impressed and says, 'He's a fantastic player.' I give him a look. Two days previously we had been looking at this diary so now he adds, 'or she, I don't know which.' Anneli is listening attentively.

Christa and I are going to the Engadine with Anneli and Schorschi. When we make a stop on the way I find a hairslide in the car park. Both the children show interest in it and want to have it (Schorschi has the longer and thicker hair). Christa says quite spontaneously, 'Oh, look Schorschi, Anneli can have this for her hair.' There's no really good reason for this and the slide will never stay in Anneli's ringlets. Schorschi is disappointed and wants it nevertheless, but Anneli now insists on having it. The point for both children: interest in dressing one's hair is a matter for girls.

Christa tells the *Wide World Story* by Marie Marcks, in which the main character is a girl. When she shows them the first picture, Christa explains to Schorschi, who has never heard the story before, that the figure in the picture, who is wearing trousers, is a girl. She asks him, 'Isn't she pretty, Schorschi?' and then answers the question herself, saying 'She's a pretty girl, isn't she?' Then she goes on and Schorschi echoes, 'Pretty girl.'

In the evening Christa and Anneli and Schorschi look at a book by Tomi Ungerer, *Alumette*, in which once again the main character is a girl. Again Christa asks Schorschi, 'Isn't that a pretty girl?'

I notice that in both cases Christa directs her questions to Schorschi, although she is reading with both children and Anneli could also have been asked whether the girl is pretty. But in this way the 'little man' is encouraged to make a judgement about the appearance of a woman, and this on the very first page of the book, before anything has been said about the character and what she is doing. And all this in the presence of a girl. Thus a boy learns early to judge women by outward appearance. Later on in life he may meet women to whom he is in every way inferior, but he will still be able to judge her from her appearance and make her look silly. And the girl is learning to accept this.

30 March 1984 (2 years 7 months)

I always used to think that girls' being encouraged earlier than boys to help their mothers with the housework was a tale of sexist upbringing in the past. But everyday life was to put me right.

Christa, Schorschi, Anneli and I are still in the Engadine. Since Anneli is already well able to take her half empty plate and cutlery from the table I say without thinking after our evening meal, 'Oh, Anneli, bring me the plates, there's a good girl.' She does so.

Schorschi is romping around somewhere. I praise Anneli, 'Thank you, Anneli, you are a good girl helping me, aren't you?'

Christa wants to ask a favour of our landlady. Since Anneli speaks more clearly than Schorschi, she's the one who's given this task. Christa says to her, 'Anneli, be a good girl and go to Frau G., bring up some wool and tell her we'll need the big bath tub for you and Schorschi.' Anneli does so. Once again she's been a very good girl and we tell her so. She's really pleased with herself.

Schorschi can't do this and therefore does not have to 'be good' like Anneli and help us. So he doesn't get accustomed so early to being 'a good boy', and expecting praise for it. He doesn't get used to housework so early, either, but sees this as a girl's task.

Are women more circumspect, friendly and helpful because they were taught to be so much earlier in life than boys?

2 April 1984 (2 years 8 months)

We're at a gymnastics class for mothers and children. Martin, a boy the same age as Anneli but bigger and stronger, keeps taking her ball that they're supposed to be playing a particular game with.

First he goes up to her and grabs hold of the ball. She yells and tries desperately to keep hold of it, bracing herself and bending over with feet firm, clutching the ball in front of her. Finally she scolds him, saying he shouldn't do this. But she doesn't manage to hang on to the ball – not surprisingly, for he's bigger and with one good shove the ball is his. All the mothers and other children are sitting in a circle watching, including Martin's mother. I'm absolutely seething, but since there's an unwritten law among mothers that says you shouldn't tell a child off in front of its own mother I don't say anything, either. I haven't the nerve to tell Martin off. Having lost the struggle Anneli stands there frustrated and looking daggers at Martin – who in the meantime is sitting on the ball, his legs apart, looking really pleased with himself and oozing self-satisfaction and superiority, his pose identical with that of hundreds of pictures of men.[37] There's an air of embarrassment in the group, with all of us still sitting there watching. Martin's mother feels she has to do something to make up for Anneli's disappointment, so she offers her another ball, saying, 'Here you are, you can have mine.' Hesitantly Anneli goes up to her, takes the ball and starts to play again.

Now the whole incident is repeated. Martin takes the new ball from Anneli, although from the very start she has been trying to hide it behind her back. The same scene occurs and at the end she gets another ball from Martin's mother, who doesn't say a word to Martin. Then it all happens a third time. His mother makes excuses for him and when he refuses to give the ball back again says he's going through a stubborn phase. Apart from this one comment his behaviour is absolutely accepted by his mother, who gives him no other indication at all of her displeasure.

Anneli's the one who's kept waiting and who has to make do with something new. Although she only wants to get on with playing quietly she has to suit her mood to meet the boy's aggression, to come to terms with defeat, to get used to the substitute plaything and then to start her game again. This requires quite a bit of adaptation to masculine behaviour, whereas absolutely nothing is expected of the boy. He's fine the way he is.

No one seems at all bothered about the girl's psyche. Far from it – the interests of the girl, who might also happen to be going through a stubborn phase, are completely ignored. She learns that basically boys are always right and that she's the one who has to adjust; she soon learns she may as well abandon any idea of wanting anything for herself.

The following principle, formulated by Rousseau over two hundred years ago is apparently as valid as it ever was: 'Train them [girls] to break off their games and return to other occupations without a murmur. Habit is all that is needed . . . this habitual restraint produces a docility which woman requires all her life long, for she will always be in subjection to a man, or to man's judgement, and she will never be free, to set her own opinion over his.'[38]

3 April 1984 (2 years 8 months)

Anneli is fiddling with the door key underneath the chair and when she's finished she says she's repaired the chair just like Hans did the house. Why didn't a woman's name occur to her when she said repair?

We're at the Free Music Centre in Munich – part of the local alternative scene – at a course in music and movement for three-year-olds. There are four other girls, a boy and six mothers there. The course leader is a man. A story is read from a picture book and is then reinterpreted in music and movement. We all stand in a row and sing 'I'm little Balthazar and I'm not afraid' – five girls, six women, one boy and one man. I notice that Anneli, who has recently been struggling with the definitions of girl and boy and what she herself is, is puzzled. Why has the course leader, who knew beforehand how many girls there were to be in the class, selected a story with a boy as the main character and then had them all sing it? Typical lack of thought, that is, the absolute inability to think in any other than masculine terms of definition. We're all so firmly entrenched in this system of masculine presumption that we hardly ever notice it. But it's inconceivable for a boy to define himself as a girl! Just imagine six fathers, five boys, one woman and a girl singing, 'I'm little Barbara and I feel really scared.'

7 April 1984 (2 years 8 months)

When I'm dressing Anneli in the morning I happen to see a skirt in the cupboard that Anneli was given some time ago and I put it on her. She looks really pretty and she herself likes it. All day long I keep noticing that she seems different – because she's not wearing trousers. She's a pretty little girl that I can't help connecting with all those typically feminine charactersitics, of being vulnerable, fragile and in need of care and protection. When we go shopping and for a walk I keep wanting to take hold of her hand, a thing I don't normally do. And I want to take her in my arms and give her a kiss and a cuddle more often than usual. It all goes to show how important gender specific clothing is in defining the interaction of children and adults.

In the afternoon we're visiting a family with a son who's five months younger. Here again appeals are made to the boy to behave like a gentleman when they start squabbling about a toy he's taken from her.

9 April 1984 (2 years 8 months)

A few days ago Anneli was with Claudia, who's seven, and her friends. Today she suddenly asks me to plait her hair and put slides in it. In contrast to her usual self she keeps wanting to have her hair done and takes care not to disarrange it. She keeps looking at herself in the mirror and is worried if one of the slides seems to be missing. I assume she's got this from Claudia. So far I hadn't thought about how much influence older children have on younger ones, being of course much more fixed in their roles.

Grandma is here. In the evening she happens to mention that she's thinking of getting Anneli a doll's pram. Klaus tries to dissuade her, fearing that she'll spend even more time playing with dolls. Grandma turns to me and says, 'Are you trying to turn her into a boy? Girls ought to play with dolls and they need a doll's pram to wheel around. If you're not careful she'll turn into a real tomboy, more like a boy than a girl. It's not right, and if you won't get her these things then I will.'

I'm unable to continue the conversation because I can hear Anneli yelling somewhere, but I'm surprised at how clearly my mother, who has never read a book on gender specific upbringing, describes the forming of character by the environment, according to how parents interpret the sex of their child.

10 April 1984 (2 years 8 months)

At the music centre – the same scenario as last week, but with a different story and the same cast for the 'tragedy' (that's how I see it). What do we sing this time? 'I'm the little hevel*mann*'* This is what girls are taught; no wonder we women are plunged into identity crises, we were never allowed to develop one, and still aren't.

That this irritates Anneli and that she's not indifferent to the definition as girl or boy is clear from the angry and aggressive tone she speaks in to an old woman who had addressed her as a boy in the street immediately afterwards.

13 April 1984 (2 years 8 months)

Schorschi is going to the hairdresser's with Christa and we go with them. The hairdresser says she's amazed his hair's so long and that it's not the right thing for a boy. When she's finished she says with great satisfaction to Schorschi, 'There you are, now you look like a boy again.'

In the evening the children are out with Klaus. When they come home they have to take their shoes off straight away as they've been to a farm. Anneli can do this, so she takes off her own shoes and then helps Klaus. I didn't really teach her this, she picked it up herself. Schorschi can't quite manage, so now Anneli kneels down in front of Schorschi, who is sitting on the stairs holding his feet out to her, and starts taking his shoes off, explaining to him how to do it. I have often heard and have read in books that girls tend to wait on boys and often know more about their brothers' things than the boys themselves. Is this how it starts? It begins with the quick child learning these things better and demonstrating them with understandable pride. Then she's encouraged by her mother to carry on, because it means things get done more quickly and is a great help in the home.

The boy's honour is in no way affected by this because it's only in the rarest of cases that a girl can set a boy an example where it matters. So it develops into a traditional domestic ritual and in the course of life the girl's talent is turned into being eternally responsible for others, especially men. What starts out as an advantage finishes up as exactly the opposite.

The Little Hevelmann is a bedtime story addressed to a little boy. (*Translator's note*.)

15 April 1984 (2 years 8 months)
Anneli and I are at Elizabeth and Martin's. Among the games I find 'Happy Families' and have a look at it.

Girls are represented as follows: in a mackintosh with an umbrella, in a long lace nightdress with a doll on her lap, painting, shopping, on a swing, playing with a ball, playing in the sand, with the bears, skating in a short skirt, hanging out washing, playing a recorder, holding a rabbit and stroking it, going for a walk, wearing an apron and carrying in cakes, lying in bed.

Boys are shown doing the following: taking a dog for a walk, carrying washing, building a snowman, building sandcastles, playing football, fishing, as a painter, beating a drum, driving a scooter, as a chimney sweep, as a chef, in the rain without an umbrella, rambling with a rucksack, stick and hat, going shopping with a basket.

The difference is obvious – the only thing girls and boys have in common is shopping.

One of Martin's friends, Oliver, who is four, is also there. Oliver is not as confident or as well co-ordinated in speech and movement as Anneli, as his father himself says to me. All the children need to have a pee. The boys stand and I restrain Anneli. Then Oliver calls in a contemptuous tone, 'Oh, look at her, she's a girl.' Anneli gets fidgety, is not able to pass water and insists on standing. She only manages when the boys have gone.

Oliver has obviously picked up this tone of contempt for girls somewhere, and he's well aware of his own worth in spite of his weaknesses – all because he can pee standing up. This is just like those stupid situations at work in later life. A woman may do what she will; she will never be allowed to be as good as a man. This programme's already running in our children's brains. The scene has made quite an impression on Anneli and has upset her, and for several days she has problems passing water.

16 April 1984 (2 years 8 months)
Schorschi and Anneli are in the car talking, for no apparent reason, about their mothers' bosoms and about how big or small those of children are. Both of them emphasise the importance of bosoms and insist that they themselves have one, including Schorschi. They often play 'bosoms' and I realise that breasts are very important to

Breast envy.

children, at least as much if not more so than a penis. Not only have the children been occupied with this subject, I have, too, and I discover that Freud did recognise and discuss the phenomenon of breast envy but that it was not taken up in works easily accessible to the non-expert. Why is so much time devoted to penis envy?

17 April 1984 (2 years 8 months)

We're having our evening meal. The children are drinking mineral water, I nothing and Klaus beer. The children are talking and Anneli is explaining to Schorschi that her Daddy is a teacher (he teaches once a week). Schorschi says, 'Your Mummy's a teacher as well,' to which Anneli responds, 'No, she's a teacher's wife.'

From gymnastics classes and visits to school she knows what a teacher is. I'm dismayed by her utterance and join in, telling them I'm a teacher sometimes (one or two classes!). Only then does Anneli accept what Schorschi says. To her I am principally the wife of a man with a profession.

After the meal the children suddenly decide they want a drink of beer. So I pour a little alcohol-free beer into their glasses. They toast one another and are enormously pleased with their own importance. Anneli says, 'Now we're men' and Schorschi echoes, 'Just like men.' When I ask them why they say, 'Because we're drinking beer.'

Is every little thing picked up by children? Including the fact that I rarely drink beer, although no one has ever said anything about it? I wouldn't have thought that children would draw conclusions about the differences between men and women because of this one point.

19 April 1984 (2 years 8 months)

On our way to Berlin Anneli is imitating animal noises, including a lamb and all its family. The lamb has a very high voice and utters pathetic sounding little whimpers; Mother Sheep is just the same; but Daddy has a deep firm voice. I encourage her to do the whole lot again and the second time she varies Mother Sheep's voice somewhat, making it sound a little less tearful. The third time is just like the first. Child and mother are classed together, but the father is different.

22 April 1984 (2 years 8 months)
We are at an exhibition. One of the exhibits is a photomontage by a
woman, called 'Memory of Nina and Nik'. Nina is represented by
a little pleated dress for a baby and a little garland of flowers for
the head. A pair of rompers, a little knitted hat and a wooden rattle
with three wooden balls symbolise the boy. It's not surprising that
the theorists say boys get different toys from girls from the very
start; in this case the girl doesn't get one at all, there is only a
decoration of flowers – but, as we know, she has an innate craving
for decorative effects!

In the afternoon we drive out to one of the lakes near Berlin, the
Wannsee. Motor cycles are simply whipping past us. Anneli is just
as fascinated by them as she was a year ago. Like all children. She
says, 'When I grow up and I'm a man, Mummy, I'll be able to
drive a motorbike, won't I, and I'll go brrrmmmmm,
brrrrrmmmmm . . . '

Obviously the things she noticed last year have borne fruit. The
classification of motorbikes as masculine has stuck in her mind
and, if she really wants to drive one later on, it's an idea that will
have to be overcome – or she can forget about it.

26 April 1984 (2 years 8 months)
The children are turning up at playgroup in ones and twos. It's still
early. They sit in the sandpit with some of the parents around,
chatting. The subject is toys, in particular, Duplo pieces.

One mother, Annegret, says it's a pity there are so few human
figures in the sets. We try to list the men in their various functions:
the driver of the dredger, the farmer, the garage attendant . . . etc.
It turns out that two of the little figures are supposed to be female,
since they have blond hair and plaits. 'Well, fancy that' – we're all
surprised. Annegret remarks, 'Somehow I always knew that there
were supposed to be two female figures in there somewhere, but I
wasn't quite sure; I always talk about the "little men", even when
I mean the women.' And she asks, 'I wonder why?' Everyone else
says they do the same.

I don't know why either. Except that the world is principally
comprised of men – even among emancipated women at a Berlin
playgroup.

How can a boy help but think he's a member of the controlling group. Even in these 'harmless' Duplo pieces the 'atmosphere' is there which makes strong men of tender little babies.

6 May 1984 (2 years 9 months)
I always seem to say grandad and grandma, the farmer and his wife, husband and wife, boy and girl, etc., just like a talking machine that has been programmed always to put the male partner first. Only since I've been paying attention to my speech patterns have I become conscious of how I use language. No doubt I learned from my mother, as Anneli is learning from me, always to put the man first. Yet another way in which masculine dominance is created, without there being any achievement to justify it.

7 May 1984 (2 years 9 months)
A woman friend of mine from Bavaria, a self-confident, down-to-earth farmer, has come to visit us in Berlin. After she has been getting ready to go out one evening Anneli suddenly asks her, 'When I grow up, will I be a woman as well?'

Ottilie says simply, 'Yes.'

To which Anneli then responds, 'When I grow up, will I be a man or only a woman?'

Ottilie's spontaneous rejection of this statement is blunt: 'Goodness gracious! What's "only" supposed to mean? That's a fine thing, I must say. Where d'you pick up rubbish like that?'

I'm delighted with Ottilie's indignation and at her response. She quite spontaneously gave Anneli the only correct and appropriate answer. I wonder if it will stick?

9 May 1984 (2 years 9 months)
A friend of mine, Sabine, wants to sit Anneli on her lap. In a high pitched, ingratiating tone of voice she says, turning to Anneli and stretching out her arms, 'Come on, poppet, come and sit on Auntie Sabine's lap.' Our glances happen to meet. We have just been talking about my diary and it made Sabine really angry. She lets her arms drop, changes her pose, and instead of stretching out to Anneli, leans back and says, quite neutrally, 'Do you want to come and sit on my knee or would you rather go on running around?' Quite a difference, isn't there?

11 May 1984 (2 years 9 months)
David drags a book by Janosch over to me. Anneli and he want me
to read to them from it. It describes men on a farm chopping wood,
carrying things around, driving tractors (again) and mother
hanging out the washing. I read:

> The ball, the ball comes flying out
> And mother hangs the washing out
> The father calls out to his son
> Who comes and puts the harness on
> The horses . . .

I surprise myself: I read the first two lines quite normally and in a
cheerful voice, but with the third line my voice becomes deeper
and I speak more slowly and ponderously. Of course; now I'm
talking about a man and a boy.

Later on I'm sitting at the typewriter but David wants to play
with me. I give him paper and pencil and am about to tell him to
draw some little men. More little men. I choke this back and then
for a moment can't think of anything to say. What should I say
instead of little men? Little women? I avoid the problem and tell
him to draw babies instead.

13 May 1984 (2 years 9 months)
On the Berlin urban motorway once again there are hundreds of
motorbikes in front of us, behind us, overtaking us. Anneli is
spellbound. Two days ago she saw an act at the circus with two
bears riding a motorbike and since then she has been especially
fascinated by motorbikes with two people on them. Every time we
see one she says, 'The man sits at the front and the woman sits
behind, holding on to him.' When she sees a motor cyclist without
a female passenger she says, 'He's driving without a woman.' In
response to my comment that it might be a woman driving she
says, 'No, 'cos he's got a black crash helmet.'

I remember an especially splendid specimen of masculinity
Anneli saw a few days ago when she stood admiring a BMW and
watching its owner making himself ready to depart with great
pomp and circumstance, putting on a black crash helmet. For
children gender categorisation is composed of such details.

She is still prattling on about motor cycles and sits on the central gear channel in the car and goes 'bbrrmmm, bbbrrrrmmmmmm'. I tell her that she can ride a motorbike when she grows up. She chatters on 'Yes, then Jonathan [her special friend from play-group] 'n' me'll go real fast, when we're grown up and men. With black crash helmets.' When I tell her she can also do that if she's a woman she says indignantly, 'No, Mummy, we'll be men. I'll go with Jonathan from playgroup and I'll sit at the front. We're men.'

When she was getting dressed this morning she assured me she was going to be a woman. Apparently her sex wishes change with the activities she fancies, all of which are categorised according to gender. I feel cross. There are enough women in Berlin nowadays riding motorbikes. So why can't we manage to break out of the traditional ways of thinking?

15 May 1984 (2 years 9 months)
We arrive at the playgroup, late as usual. They're all in the garden standing around the old car which has just been renovated and has to be put back together again. Regine, the teacher (female), and Utz, the welfare attendant (male), are standing next to one another. Utz starts work on the car to get it going to drive the kids to the park. Anneli asks when it will be ready. I tell her to ask Utz. Why do I say Utz and not Regine? This teaches Anneli that if a woman and a man are both present the man is senior, the one who will give information. He has the facts and questions are to be addressed to him. In this way women and girls early on become accustomed to the typical speech habit of expressing themselves in questions.

I discuss different approaches to girls and boys at playgroup with Regine and Utz. Utz admits he thinks girls are more sensitive and that this is probably because of the way he thinks of women. For this reason he is particularly gentle and kind to girls, both in the way he talks and the way he plays with them.

17 May 1984 (2 years 9 months)
On the way home Anneli is chattering away to herself in the car.

'Mummy, you haven't been to high school yet, because you haven't got a satchel; before when I was little and a girl I didn't go to school either, but when I'm a bigger boy I'll go to high school and then I'll have a satchel.'

Being bigger, being able, being allowed, all this is connected with the male sex. I'm not aware of personal blame – or maybe I am when I think of the old car at the playgroup.

19 May 1984 (2 years 9 months)

Klaus has been with Anneli to the playground not far from the flat. There are two other children there about the same age as Anneli. Both of them have plaits. When Anneli asks them their names it becomes apparent that one of them is a boy. It is the first time I'm aware of a boy with a feminine trait in public; it must be Berlin, I think.

A man of quite normal appearance, about 40, comes to the playground. He jokes with the children a bit, addressing the two children with plaits as girls. Inevitably he asks Anneli whether she's a girl or a boy. She says, 'I'm a boy,' and he actually takes her hand and says, 'Congratulations.' (Anneli is well aware what this means, from various birthday celebrations.) Later on she goes up to him of her own accord and says, 'I'm a girl really.' He won't believe it, contradicting her with some vehemence and saying she can't be because she doesn't look like a girl. So is self-esteem developed.

There are several couples sitting around the playground. The women talk to the children as they go past and watch what's going on. All the men are reading, their lack of interest in events around them obvious from their bearing and manner. They clearly do not feel part of this world of women and children. So children get the message that men are always occupied with important matters beyond their experience, but that women are like children, living in the same world.

20 May 1984 (2 years 9 months)

Again and again I come up against the discrepancy between the real world with all its sexisms and disadvantages for little girls and the world of the stories and explanations I tell Anneli. This is the world I dream of. Why do I lie to her?

I think of traditional ideas of bringing up children and of morality. Weren't we, the generation of the 1950s, presented with a world different from reality? Hasn't it always been normal to give children one is bringing up a picture of the world as adults would like it to be? Wasn't it so in traditional forms of upbringing that there was a contradiction between the ideal presented to children and the reality? Then I think of Christian teaching and forget my qualms of conscience.

At breakfast Anneli says, 'Now I've eaten so much, now I'll get fat and then I'll be a man.'

I reply, 'Daddy isn't fat. Why do you think men are fat?'

She takes refuge in the comment, 'But stupid men are fat.'

I hadn't really noticed that in our society men are the more weighty ones. I notice men in the street – Anneli's right.

Again the child has connected an item of outer appearance with sex. Since she hasn't yet learned that sex is permanent, she imagines it can be altered according to appearance and activity. She realises that the sexes have differing characteristics laid down in definite rules. The cardinal principle, that it is superficial external attributes not the actual sexual characteristics that determine gender, is already firmly fixed in her mind.

25 May 1984 (2 years 9 months)

Anneli and I are visiting a friend of mine, a teacher, at her holiday kindergarten. I am surprised to see that with one exception there are only boys there. I ask her why there are only boys in her group and she answers, 'Well, it's always the same during the holidays – mothers only send boys to kindergarten so they'll have a bit of peace at home. The boys get too excited at home, and make a mess and don't do as they're told. It's different with girls; they're not so wild. It's easier to have them at home; there's no mess and they might even give their mothers a hand with the housework as well, or at least see what it's like – for later on.' When I ask her why she assumes this to be the case, she says, 'I'm not assuming. Mothers tell me that's how it is when they bring the boys along or explain why they're not bringing the girls.'

While we're talking about this she's trying a little overall of felt with a matching pointed cap on her daughter. I ask Kathrin, aged four and a half, what this pretty costume is for. Her mother interrupts, saying, 'It's not for Kathrin, it's for our summer fête at the kindergarten. The children in my group are going as dwarves, but since the boys here won't stand still long enough for me to try their things on, Kathrin does it for them. Don't you, Kathrin? There's a good girl, helping Mummy.'³⁹

Kathrin nods and stands there patiently, while the 15 or so boys whose costumes she is trying on are prancing around enjoying themselves.

Anneli is there watching and listening.

1 June 1984 (2 years 10 months)
Anneli and I are off to the farm in the South Tyrol once again. When we arrive only Frau Gärtner is there to welcome us; both husband and children are out. So Anneli comes with me up to our room. When she hears the children's voices a little later she decides to go straight down to the kitchen on her own. By now she's familiar enough with the rooms and the people on the farm.

But a few minutes later she creeps back into the room, looking rather subdued. When I ask her why she says, 'I didn't go in, Mummy, there's a man there and I daren't.' I then envisage some formidable South Tyrolean about the house and, full of understanding, I go down with her.

It turns out it's simply the farmer himself sitting at the kitchen table with his family. She was frightened of him! I was going to make a joke of this with Anneli, but then I remembered something Bernadette had said when we were leaving last time about two months ago. She had whispered in Anneli's ear, 'But next time you come, don't bring your Dada with you. I don't like him 'cos he scares me.' And that was Anneli's father who is certainly not at all formidable and who had spent a lot of time playing with the kids. The last time we had arrived all together Anna, too, after showing delight with Anneli and me, withdrew on seeing Klaus.

I remember my own childhood. It was very easy going and pleasant playing with other children, as long as only their mother was there. As soon as their father turned up I began to feel uneasy and the mood was spoiled, we no longer felt so familiar and uninhibited. Authority was lurking in the background, even though it may never have been demonstrated. The man was a disruptive element. Usually we prefered to abandon the game and go home.

Obviously children feel unfamiliarity, respect or even fear in the presence of men who do not belong to the immediate family circle.

I then begin to reconsider my own behaviour in this respect. Doesn't it happen sometimes when under pressure that little threats slip out, 'If you're not careful Herr G. will be angry,' or 'Perhaps we shouldn't do that, Herr G. might not like it.'

These statements fit the way I feel myself when I'm with the children. I know that whatever mess the children make Frau G. will understand and will sort it out. But I'm not quite sure about her husband; I feel just as slightly insecure and slightly uncomfortable when he's there and I have children with me, just like in my own childhood. But with his wife I feel quite at ease; I know how she's going to react.

It's different, of course, when I'm on my own with him or only in the company of adults – in the evening, for example. Then I'm completely relaxed and at ease, and talk with him as an equal (he's six years younger than me). That is, quite normally. It's only when children I am responsible for are present that I feel I shouldn't bother him any more than necessary; I want to be unobtrusive and withdraw with the children. I'm on the children's side and I identify with them.

Is it, then, my own attitude that gives the children the idea that men are formidable? Do other women do the same? How else does fear of men develop – especially in small girls?

2 June 1984 (2 years 10 months)
Once again we're buying shoes in Bolzano. Because of her long curls everyone addresses her quite naturally as a girl. So what, I think. In the shoe shop all the assistants have something to say to Anneli and when she says it's her birthday soon, they immediately respond, 'Are you going to get a new doll?' Then the new doll is described in detail. So far dolls haven't really played such a very big role in Anneli's life, but the following day, when another stranger happens to ask her what she wants for her birthday, she says at once 'A doll.'

I very much doubt that's what she really wants and am fed up at the way complete strangers pin certain wishes and preferences on to a child just on the basis of its appearance, though the child itself may be totally uninterested. Somewhere along the way the oft praised 'human being' gets lost. But I'm determined that Anneli shan't be subject to such stupid fixations about what is typical for girls: the curls will have to go.

Anneli urgently needs a new blouse for the summer. In the shop we are shown blouses with frills, in white, in satin and in all sorts of other impractical colours and patterns. Do people think girls never eat spaghetti or mess around in the dirt? I ask to see some boys' shirts. The saleswoman ignores my request three times and then points out that the buttons are the wrong way round – a major problem as far as she's concerned. But the colours and the patterns of the boys' shirts are so drab that I go without.

3 June 1984 (2 years 10 months)
In the evening an aunt comes and cuts Bernadette's, now five, Anna's, three, and Anneli's hair very short. The children have a whale of a time and are delighted with their new hairstyles. Anneli says with relief, 'Now it won't tug when it's combed.' That's true.

All the other adults on the farm are appalled at their short hair. The girls are told over and over again they look like boys. The farmer, the father of the three girls, says to them, 'Well, at least you looks like lads now even if you're not.' During the next few days, whenever they're feeling particularly good, they say, 'Now we're lads,' and then they play 'being boys' for ages, that is, they dash around as they always do when they're in particularly high spirits. 'Being boys' certainly comes to mean something special for the girls.

And so it happens that boys and men, without any effort at all on their own part, become highly esteemed creatures to girls. Adults make this possible with all their predetermined value judgements.

After our evening meal Anneli comes running up to me bubbling over, 'I've eaten so much that I'll be as big as a man.' Becoming a boy or a man is a very desirable goal in the life of a little girl.

4 June 1984 (2 years 10 months)
I'm out in the mountains with the three children. Surprisingly, they can manage rambles lasting several hours as long as they're having a jolly time.

I'm surprised that Bernadette and Anna never fail to take their dolls with them on these excursions. Even when Anna, the younger of the two, simply forgets hers or doesn't want to take it because Anneli, whom she likes to imitate, isn't taking one, then her five-year-old sister reminds her, and the doll comes along too.

Not once have they tried to pass the dolls over to me, however difficult the going gets over stones and roots or through tangled growth across slopes and streams – they always have their dolls tight in their arms like a part of their own bodies. Is it this early practice that makes it easier for these women later on to endure always having a child in their arms – better than I do, for example? The elder sister always makes sure the younger one doesn't drop out. Children are known to bring one another up.[40]

One afternoon Bernadette teaches the two younger girls a song she learned at kindergarten. It tells how 'mamma cradles the bairn' and 'dadda works in the forest', etc., etc. And the refrain, which they all sing, goes, ' . . . and that's how a family should be.'

Once again I'm surprised at the way in which the ideology of the nuclear family permeates the child's imagination; how much educational institutions are helped by the children in their care; how great an influence this early teaching has on the children of preschool age.

We're sitting in a meadow acting out fairy tales according to the children's fantasies. They choose roles they like for themselves. Bernadette wants to be the good queen, Anneli the motor cyclist and Anna also a motor cyclist. But Bernadette intervenes here with her sister who, she says, can't be anything but a princess. Anna can't make up her mind. Bernadette tells her what to do once again and that's the end of Anna's one attempt to be independent. Anneli, thank goodness, still sticks to her motor cyclist.

6 June 1984 (2 years 10 months)

Anneli urgently needs a blouse, since the weather is getting warmer and we only have warm clothes with us. I go into a shop with Anneli – without curls – simply indicate her, and say, 'We'd like something to go with jeans in this warmer weather.'

The shop assistant asks, 'A check for everyday wear or something a bit smarter?'

That's more to the point – quite a difference from all the lovely expensive girls' blouses we were shown last time without even being asked – now that Anneli passes for a boy.

7 June 1984 (2 years 10 months)

We're walking in the Sahrn Valley. Anneli looks at the snow-covered mountains and says, 'We can't go up there, only men can.'

When I ask her whether women can't go up there as well, she answers, 'No, not with Anna and me.' Aha, so women are connected with children, and what children can't do women can't do either. Then she emphasises once again that only men can do that. In response to my comment that I've been climbing in the high mountains more often than Daddy she says, 'But with Anna and me and you you can't. Women don't do that, just people.'

I'm speechless at that. So there are men and people, who can do all sorts of things, and women and children, who can't.

8 June 1984 (2 years 10 months)

The three children and I go for a walk to a lovely play area in the woods. Bernadette rushes over at once to the double swing. This is more important to her than anything and she doesn't even want to go with us to the nearby café to buy an ice cream.

The two smaller children find the idea of an ice cream more tempting, so we bring one for Bernadette as well. But she won't abandon the swing to eat her ice cream and quite calmly watches me starting to eat the ice cream intended for her. It's all very quiet, but then suddenly we hear the sound of children's voices and three boys of about six or seven come bounding into the play area.

As soon as Bernadette sees them she stops the swing and leaps from it in haste. She runs over to me, looking insecure and apprehensive. Without so much as a glance in our direction one of the boys gets on to the swing and shouts to the others to join him. I'm standing right next to the swing with the three girls. Bernadette has barely got off it when it's taken over by this six-year-old without any hesitation at all. He doesn't waver for a second, doesn't ask any questions, doesn't show a moment's doubt about who's in charge of the swing now.

I'm incensed. When I take hold of the swing, pointing out that Bernadette wants to finish her turn, he ignores me and calls all the louder to the others to hurry up. We're no more than fresh air to him. I try to persuade Bernadette to get up again, telling her I'm there to help and that the other children can wait until she's had her go. But wild horses wouldn't drag her back on to that swing. And the two smaller children, who had been waiting patiently for their turn, no longer dare to have a go. In the face of one six-year-old boy none of my girls wants to follow her original wish. Despite my presence none of them wants to risk a confrontation with the boy.

Since I obviously can't force them to and also don't want us to stand there admiring these mini machos I find something else to interest the girls and we leave. In the meantime the swing has been taken over by all three boys. In a matter of seconds the play area has been occupied by men and is therefore more than full.

This little scene seems to me to represent in miniature the reality of the society we live in.

A man turns up in a place occupied by a woman. He ignores her, giving no indication he so much as notices she's there. At the first sign of his impending arrival she makes way for him. She doesn't force him to take notice of her and avoids any confrontation. She just gets out of his way, leaving for him the prime spots and cushy jobs. A given number of men needs more space than the same number of women.

I feel like bursting into tears and can only hope that the children haven't really understood what was going on. They had stood by watching carefully. How many situations like this has Bernadette already witnessed to make her react as quickly as she did in accordance with the masculine ethos?

Poor kids. I felt sorry for them in the future and was furious. I explained the situation to them by saying that it just showed how stupid the boys were, that they didn't even know you had to wait until the other children had finished their turn. I wonder how much effect words can have as against events?

12 June 1984 (2 years 10 months)
Brilliant sunshine. After their afternoon nap I want to take the children for a walk. But they don't really want to; they would prefer to sit in the living room with their dolls – that is, Bernadette has decided they would.

After some discussion, however, they are persuaded to walk at least as far as the play area, on condition they can take their dolls with them. Naïvely I agree. This is the first time Anneli has also taken her doll on a walk. The whole caboodle gathers outside the farm: the children, the dolls and the prams, Anneli this time with her own pram for her doll. We look like a regular mother's outing.

All the dolls are carefully strapped in. We make slow progress. The play area is in the wood and it's quite hard work for the children, but patiently and with considerable effort they push, tug and lift the prams over stones, roots, cart ruts and holes. Anneli, too, is toiling away. I walk behind the children and it's a sad sight seeing what difficulties they have getting their prams through the wood.

Anneli is the first one to lose patience, but I have no intention of pushing her pram for her. She has to see for herself why she is not able – as she would really like and as her legs are itching to – to hop, skip, run and hide. She finally gets thoroughly fed up, throws the pram and the doll over and runs off. Now she's an absolute bundle of energy in comparison with before, radiant with delight, release and self-confidence.

Anna and Bernadette are still pushing their prams along – I've ended up with Anneli's after all. It is as though the children are chained to walking frames; with their hands firmly on the handles, eyes on the ground looking for obstacles, all their concentration directed to the prams. This takes up all their energy and interest and they walk along dutifully. All the strength of their small bodies is directed into pushing the prams.

In contrast it's striking how Anneli, having left the pram to its fate, moves freely, seeing and picking things up, playing with all manner of objects in this short time. Beetles, flowers, stones, sticks, herbs, snails, worms: a host of exciting things laying claim to her attention. But Bernadette and Anna have no energy for all of this; they don't even see them.[41]

13 June 1984 (2 years 10 months)

It's Sunday and we've come out to an idyllically situated little lake where the children love to play on their own. There are a lot of people there today and the children hardly play at all but spend their time watching people. When I observe more carefully I realise they are not watching 'people', but men, for they are the only ones doing anything worth watching. They hop, dive, swim, jump, play ball or football, run. The women, sit, lie, sunbathe, occasionally one will scream as a man splashes water over her and very occasionally one will risk going for a swim. But this doesn't attract much attention since the women slide quietly into the water. Me too; I simply sit on the boat jetty, keeping an eye on the children and sunbathing. I get into conversation with other bathers and am several times asked the inevitable question, in front of the children, 'Have you come on holiday on your own?' Without your husband? With three children I don't really feel that I'm 'on my own'. Had my husband been accompanying me apparently I wouldn't have been. I wonder whether the children interpret that to mean that without a man at her side a woman is incomplete.

14 June 1984 (2 years 10 months)

Anneli has burnt her hand a little on the hotplate and is crying miserably. I let her cry but after about half an hour I tell her that Schorschi didn't cry nearly as much when his head had to be stitched by the doctor. She pauses for a minute, looking at me. But Grandma butts in, 'Well, Schorschi's a boy.'

I see a flash in Anneli's eye; she looks at me with satisfaction and starts crying again.

21 June 1984 (2 years 10 months)

A playground in Berlin: Anneli is with 18-month-old Annalena and her mother. The little girl wants to climb up the slide from the bottom. She's just making her second attempt when a four-year-old boy appears at the top. As soon as we see the boy, Annalena's mother calls, 'Annalena, get out of the way, the boy wants to slide down.'

I wonder why it has to be Annalena who gives way and why the boy can't wait until Annalena makes the way clear for sliding. After all, she was there first. The same old story. As soon as a male appears, small though he may be, it's the woman or girl who has to give ground. The girl has to fit in. Mothers encourage their daughters to give ground from an early age – even when, like Annalena's mother, they are self-confident single parents well aware of at least the theoretical implications.

Since it seems to me that one child's fun is being exchanged for another's I intervene and tell him that Annalena's not moving yet. The boy looks at me incredulously, gets out at the top and begins to slide down, slowly but directly at the little girl. He glares at me as if to say, 'Now we'll see who's stronger.' I don't remove Annalena; instead I give him a good telling off and say he'd better keep out of my way. Whereupon he gives in and makes off looking rather sheepish.

I'm convinced that both little Annalena and Anneli, who is playing in the sand next to her, have got the message: they really ought
to make way when a boy appears.

25 June 1984 (2 years 10 months)
In the past few days I have noticed Anneli making the following
gestures several times: she claps her hands together, then claps her
hands on her hips, gabbles some incomprehensible words and
waves her open palms rhythmically in the air. Having seen her do
this several times and wondered what it meant, I assumed she was
imitating some ball game the girls play. When I ask her what she's
doing she says: 'I'm doing it like the girls.'
Me: 'Do you like it?'
She: 'It's because I'm a girl.'
I remember that a few weeks ago she spent a few days at Grandma's in a street where there are a lot of girls of primary school age.
Aha, so that's it! And it doesn't seem to matter whether or not she
likes it, as long as she's doing it properly, like the other girls.

She wants to be the same as the others and so she copies other
children who are just like herself defined as girls. She is not aware
she is adopting any 'feminine' behaviour in her imitation. To a
child it's all the same. She's a girl and she takes her bearings from
other girls.

26 June 1984 (2 years 10 months)
Some trifle has frightened Anneli. So I say, 'But you can't be
scared, after all, you're a girl.' I'm trying out the reverse of the
usual approach and am quite surprised at her response: 'But boys
are scared a bit.'
It is surprising how quickly children realise that the stress on a
quality in one sex implies at the same time something about the
other sex.

29 June 1984 (2 years 10 months)
Anneli has got Klaus and me to try whistling with a blade of grass
between our thumbs, just like Utz at playgroup.
Neither of us manages it at first. So she addresses herself to Klaus,
explaining to him how to do it and showing him with childish

gestures. Since Utz, who can whistle with a blade of grass, is a man she addresses herself here to another man.

When Klaus can't manage it, she turns to me and says, 'But Utz is a man just like Daddy and he could do it! But Regine couldn't.' The only phrase missing is ' . . . because she's a woman.' She didn't say it but I bet she meant it.

Anyway, I succeed in whistling quite quickly and hope I have managed to change her view of things a little.

1 July 1984 (2 years 11 months)

We're in Switzerland again. This time with Ellen and Martin (four-and-three-quarter years old). The children are delighted and happy together.

In the evening Anneli is washing her hands in the bathroom, fully concentrating on what she's doing. Martin is standing next to her, peeing into the loo. Without her having said a word to him he says, 'You can't pee standing up like me.'

Anneli turns her attention from her hands, irritated, and looks into his triumphant face. She seems uncertain. I can't restrain myself and join in, answering for Anneli, 'Of course she can. Today she peed right over an enormous rock. Don't kid yourself.'

So he says, 'She can't pee as far as I can.'

Me: 'We don't care how far you can pee' and I take Anneli, leaving him on his own.

But he won't give in, apparently needing to prove something, and follows us with his 'problem'. But since in the meantime we've started reading a beautiful book with an interesting story the subject doesn't interest Anneli any more. She doesn't listen to him.

3 July 1984 (2 years 11 months)

It's very hot for rambling and Anneli decides to run around without clothes on. She's thrilled with her body and explains that she now has got a big bosom and a big tummy because she's expecting a baby, and she sticks her tummy right out.

She becomes preoccupied with her genitals as well and giggles, she says, because it tickles. Klaus admits that the thought that his daughter's genitals are more than an organ for passing water, that they are in fact a source of pleasure, is new to him, though he'd taken this for granted with little boys. At least for him as a small boy his little penis was important to him in other ways than merely passing water, and adults, too, had attributed importance to it. He found it difficult to imagine the same to be true of his daughter. He was at a loss as to how to regard her genitals, and for this reason was unable to talk or joke about them as one did with little boys, and as he would certainly have done had she been a son.

The girl is sexless as compared with boys.

Simone de Beauvoir wrote: 'The lot of the little girl is very different. Mothers . . . feel no reverence or tenderness towards her genitals; they do not direct her attention to that secret organ . . . in a sense she has no sex organ.'[42] Apparently little has changed in human consciousness since 1949 when Simone de Beauvoir first wrote this.

4 July 1984 (2 years 11 months)

Ellen and I are talking about plans for our future life and work. I say, 'When *I* know what I want then Anneli will have to fit in with it, though of course I'm going to do my very best possible for her. But basically it's up to me, not her, and we'll manage together. It's good for her if I do what benefits me.' Ellen says that above all she'll have to decide what's best for Martin and fit her plans in with that; if she can see or imagine that something is not advantageous to him, then she simply won't do it.

Is it pure chance that the girl's mother thinks principally of herself and expects her daughter to adapt to this, whereas the boy's mother puts her son first?

While we're having our evening meal Martin suddenly says, 'Pink's a rotten colour.' Ellen interrupts him, annoyed. 'That's not true, you like pink. You're only saying that because Wasti [his seven-year-old cousin] said it and he only says it because it's a woman's colour!' Even though Ellen didn't mean to, she's established a connection between woman and inferiority.

Our conversation at table revolves around new games and adventures for Martin. These include football and camping, but he can't do either until Daddy has his holidays and can go away with him, for it's up to Daddy to teach Martin these things. Ellen is responsible for everything that goes on in the home: hobbies, reading, singing, playing music, storytelling; but Daddy is in charge of everything in the big wide world outside, for sport and action. It's not surprising the boy perceives the world as naturally being in two separate areas and that he judges girls and activities accordingly.

Ellen is knitting; suddenly she says 'Shit!' and Martin asks why. She explains that she's dropped a stitch. Martin says: 'Daddy said "shit" the last time he made a mistake typing, but that was more important, it was for the clinic.'

5 July 1984 (2 years 11 months)

Martin asks which of the two children is stronger. Ellen says he is, but that for a three-year-old girl Anneli is very strong. By putting it like this she teaches her son that girls are not *normally* strong. This won't as yet be important to Anneli, but I'm sure that as the wish to be like others increases, to be 'normal', then sentences like this will contribute to her losing her strength somewhere along the way.

Anneli and I are running hand in hand down a wide path into the village. Anneli says, 'Mummy, we're running fast now. We're the boys now, and they're just the girls.' She means Ellen and Martin; where did she get this idea from?

After the evening meal Anneli gets out one of her picture books and wants to look at it. She sits on the floor, but then along comes Martin and tries to take it away from her because *he* wants to look at it. We decide that they can look at it 'together'. The following happens.

They both lie on the floor on their stomachs with the book in front of them. Martin, the heavier, now begins gradually to push Anneli sideways so that ultimately he is lying diagonally across the book preventing Anneli from seeing anything. When he's told off he moves a few centimetres to the side – he really did give way a bit! Anneli is now *allowed* to look at the book again – although it was her idea in the first place. In this way she is able to look at short sections of the book. Neither Ellen nor I make it clear to Martin that this is not 'sharing'.

Anneli soon gets fed up with this. She gets up, fetches another book, sits down and starts to look at it, muttering to herself, 'I can get another book if Martin won't let me look.' She's showing the same reaction that is expected of and practised by grown women: giving in when a man appears and shows interest in the same thing.

The very fact that Anneli describes this as Martin not letting her do something that was really hers to do shows how fixed this idea is in her head.

Now Martin is interested in the new book she's got and the game starts from the beginning again. The girl is continually interrupted and has to adapt. But now both Ellen and I intervene. We've already spent some time discussing this diary, and I wonder whether we would otherwise have noticed what was happening.

6 July 1984 (2 years 11 months)
Mothers and children are having a rest while out on a climb. We drink tea. When Martin has emptied his beaker he throws it down in front of Anneli, who is waiting to have a drink. Ellen bends down, picks up the beaker and gives it to Anneli. She says to Martin, 'That's not the way to behave.' To me she says, 'Such thoughtlessness is typical of boys. It's just the same with grown men later in life, like when it never occurs to them to put the toilet seat back down after using it.' And it's also not necessary for them to transform this thoughtlessness into considerate thoughts if there's always a woman on hand to do her bit to avoid strife. As in Martin's case.

7 July 1984 (2 years 11 months)
I give Anneli a two-franc piece (in Switzerland) to buy chocolate. She puts it in her back pocket, commenting, 'Now I'm a boy.'
　Me: 'Why?'
　Anneli: ''Cos I've got money in my back pocket.'
　Me: 'Don't girls do that?'
　Anneli: 'No.' No further comment.
　I can't really see what she means until Ellen points out that women normally carry their money in a purse in their handbags, whereas men carry it in their trouser pockets. Obvious! It's as simple as that. But you have to be as observant as a small girl to notice things like that.

8 July 1984 (2 years 11 months)
In recent weeks Anneli has developed considerable skill in peeing while standing up, with Martin. There is no difference between the two of them in accuracy and distance of the stream. She can

press herself together and thus direct the course of the flow exactly. And they are both equally fortunate or unfortunate in hitting the toilet. Martin has at least stopped trying to make Anneli envious of his little willie.

On the other hand he is becoming more obsessed with the question as to why he doesn't have breasts and why he can't have a baby. He expands his chest, points to his ribs and assures us that's his bosom and that he does have one.

9 July 1984 (2 years 11 months)
We're looking at the barn and other outbuildings of the farm. Anneli and Martin are most fascinated by the tractor. Both of them climb up on it and play at being farmers. I say to Anneli, 'And now you're the farmer's boy.' Why didn't I say 'the farmer's girl'? You do see women driving tractors these days.

I am behind real progress and seem to live in a world of picture books when I'm talking to children.

10 July 1984 (2 years 11 months)
Anneli and Schorschi meet for the first time in ages and both are delighted. They play wild games, running up to one another shouting and boxing, enjoying the rough and tumble and testing their strength.

Then the 18-year-old (female) cousin of Schorschi, who happens to be visiting them, goes up to Anneli, takes her arm and withdraws her from the game, saying, 'Boxing and fighting aren't nice.' Schorschi stands by quite ignored and listens to Anneli being lectured for doing what he had also been doing.

In the evening Anneli starts throwing a beautiful picture book around the room. I like her to take good care of books, but when I point this out she replies, 'But boys can do it and I'm a boy.'

11 July 1984 (2 years 11 months)
I've been wondering why I still keep feeling qualms about sometimes giving Anneli a false picture of women's place in society. I'm bothering about lying and lack of fairness and feel as though I've been unjust to the other beings, that is, men, by dismissing them so readily. The problem nags at me, even making me feel guilty.

How do authors of childrens' books feel who, as we have seen, ignore whole hosts of women in certain professions? What about men who only use masculine forms of address and designations, even when they mean women? I wonder whether they ever have any twinges of conscience when they talk to their children about 'Mr Doctor',* etc.? I doubt it, so I suppress my qualms.

13 July 1984 (2 years 11 months)
I've sent Anneli out into the street to see if Klaus is coming. She's back quicker than I expect, talking about some big boys who have spat and laughed at her. At first I think she's making it up, but then Klaus comes and confirms that there are a few ten- or twelve-year-olds outside who have probably been making fun of Anneli. She had been telling the truth. I tell Anneli she should go back out and tell them off.

Anneli says she'll say 'You rotter,' or something like that. I agree and suggest she should say, 'Go away, you're stupid.' Mother and daughter are agreed. Anneli is about to set off when Klaus intervenes. He advises me not to teach her to say 'such things', saying she might well do this and have to take the consequences.

Isn't this the age old patriarchal wisdom that Klaus is passing on to his daughter, that is, that she mustn't react to masculine aggression? She should run away, flee, keep quiet, anything but seize the offensive and defend herself or even respond aggressively, if only verbally. The person who has to adjust to male aggression is the girl.

How is it possible to persuade a six-year-old girl to join a judo course to acquire greater freedom of movement for the rest of her life, if the meaning of self-defence and freedom have been educated out of her years before? Are we as grown women no longer able to give spontaneous expression to our indignation, because we have learned to fear even worse humiliation if we put the other person in his place?

Even so, Klaus had the best of intentions in wanting to protect her from these 'naughty boys'.

14 July 1984 (2 years 11 months)
In a secondhand bookshop I buy an old children's book for a friend of mine who collects them. When we get back home Anneli insists

*It is German practice to use the word 'Mr' before Doctor.

on looking at it. We look at the pictures and read it several times, without my noticing anything special about it. But Anneli asks several times, 'Why do the ladies fall in the ditch?'[43] She's right! The gentlemen, the farmers, the noblemen, all ride properly, each according to his station. But the ladies – they fall into the ditch.

As Kate Millett said, the lowest class man is always socially higher than the women of the upper classes.[44] That's what's being put across to children here. I close the book because I can't think of an explanation to give Anneli and just tell her it's a joke. But that's silly of me – at whose expense is the joke?

15 July 1984 (2 years 11 months)
Anneli and Schorschi are playing together. They want to take their clothes off, but Schorschi can't unbutton his shirt. Anneli can, so automatically I say, 'Go and undo Schorschi's buttons for him.' She does so. The usual syndrome, the domestically inadequate male doesn't have to learn to do such things, as long as some woman, either large or small, comes along to help him out.

In the course of the next few hours, when the children are running around naked, Schorschi is several times referred to affectionately by his mother as 'Little Willie'. His genitals are so obviously part of his personality that they can do instead of his name. I decide to give Anneli's genitals a name that can do for her too, and from how on I talk of her 'mary ann' which she accepts.

20 July 1984 (2 years 11 months)
Anneli is screaming with rage because she can't get her socks on. I send Schorschi across to help her. He does so, kneeling down in front of her, making an effort as she has so often done with him.

I'm strangely moved by the sight of them; it's somehow unusual and almost embarrassing. I have to hold myself back consciously from intervening and taking over from Schorschi. Is it perhaps because it's so unusual to see a 'man' waiting on a 'woman'?

25 July 1984 (2 years 11 months)
Schorschi arrives radiant and carrying his sweet little shopping basket and saying he's taking it to Grandma's, which is where we're just off to. When he arrives at Grandma's, she says, 'Hello,

Schorschi, I see you've brought your repair kit with you. But I haven't got anything to repair.'

It doesn't matter what a boy does, it's always interpreted as being something masculine, even if this is in absolute contradiction to the truth. In fact, Schorschi just enjoys taking his little shopping basket out with him.

1 August 1984 (3 years)

The little paddling pool has been put out in Grandma's garden. Anneli and Schorschi love it. They both undress quickly and Schorschi springs straight into the water. Anneli, on the other hand, approaches more cautiously and climbs in slowly, one leg after the other. Once she's tried it a few times, however, there's no holding her back. But Grandma's first comment sticks: 'Just like a girl, isn't it? – Our Anneli's so careful, but Schorschi's brave and jumps straight in.'

Schorschi's just spent three weeks at the seaside, but this is Anneli's first dip of the season.

3 August 1984 (3 years)

Anneli's playing workman with Klaus, farmer and horses with me, motorbike rider with Schorschi, doctor with Tanja and clown with Claudia. Although these professions are all common to women – except perhaps the clown – Anneli plays them all as men; I join in or listen.

When she's playing the motor cycle rider she changes completely. She lowers her voice, is more laconic, loud and peremptory than usual, and very curt. 'Hey you,' she keeps saying. When she motions to me then it is with a broad sweep of the arms; she walks with her legs apart, like John Wayne disappearing into the sunset. She is a caricature of a man but believes she is 'man' personified. Klaus doesn't like the game and lets her know it. Why not? Because it doesn't fit his idea of his sweet little girl? Schorschi's just as involved, but that doesn't bother anyone. Because it suits him!

14 August 1984 (3 years)

Ellen is again lamenting the fact that five-year-old Martin shows no interest in dolls. She sees the girls at kindergarten joining together to play doll's games and wonders why Martin doesn't do the same. But when we talk about this a bit it becomes clear that she has never played with a doll with him and never gives him any ideas as to what to do with them ('look and see if the doll's warm enough', etc.), in fact that she herself does not really believe that he could play with one as girls do. And she has never really encouraged her son to play with dolls. She admits that she has seen mothers of little girls do this: they would buy dolls' clothes together, or knit things for the dolls, take care of them and thus pass on an interest to their daughters.

Hasn't she through her reserve passed on to him the message that these objects are essentially of no interest to him?

15 August 1984 (3 years)
We're spending the weekend at a friend's farm. Anneli never watches television when we're at home, but she happens to be in the living room when the elder son is watching a film in which a woman is beaten by a man. I'm not there. She comes rushing to me in the kitchen in tears and absolutely beside herself, telling me between her sobs that a woman is being beaten. 'Why, Mummy, why can he hit her?' I can't think of an answer. My friend says, 'It's because he's a bad man.' Anneli's question as to why he is allowed to do this goes unanswered. A man does that sort of thing because he's bad.

16 August 1984 (3 years)
A neighbour is visiting us and I'm talking with her. Anneli gets bored. I'm on the point of becoming angry with her when the neighbour, seeing what's happening, points out to Anneli that her doll hasn't got any clothes on and suggests that she wash and dress it. Anneli does so and peace is maintained, even though the game with the doll doesn't last long. With a boy it would have been a car, a dredger or a building set.

Anneli must be having a bad day. Anyway we have a row. Then we keep out of one another's way until Anneli suddenly comes and says to me in her sweetest voice, 'Mummy, I'm a good girl again.' Then she goes into the garden, fetches a broom and dustpan and brush and turns to me again, saying, 'I'll clean the house for you, Mummy, and clear up, now I'll be the cleaning lady.'

I'm appalled and wouldn't have thought this sort of thing could be the result of the way I've brought her up, had it not been for an entry in this diary on 30 March 1984 which suggests the opposite. How often must I have done little things like that for them to have had this effect on Anneli? Anneli doesn't hesitate for a second in seeing a cleaner as a woman. But where on earth could I find an example of a cleaning man to correct this? I try but can only think of women cleaners. Is it my fault then that Anneli assumes that cleaning is women's work?

17 August 1984 (3 years)
In the evening Anneli and I cycle around the village a little. In a side road we see an enormous poster advertising a film and portraying a naked young woman with her hands chained and apparently hanging from a wall. There is no sign of pain or any feeling on the woman's face – she is nicely made up, her hair attractively done, and a slight smile plays on her lips.

The sight of this poster horrifies me and I try to distract Anneli so that she doesn't see it. In vain; she already has and asks, 'Mummy, why hasn't that woman got any clothes on? Why has she got chains round her hands? Has she been naughty?'

Within the space of a few days Anneli has twice encountered brutality towards women in the media. Is it possible for me to bring up my daughter to be so self-confident that this message of servile womanhood does not stick in her head, helping to form her idea of the world and her place in it?

20 August 1984 (3 years)
Grandma is visiting us again. At bedtime she urges Anneli to clear her toys away and praises her for doing so afterwards. I praise her too, of course, because it's pleasant when things are tidied up. This evening she comes over to me saying, 'Now I'll clear up and then I'll do the cleaning; I'm a good girl, aren't I, Mummy?'

Christa tells me that when she told Schorschi to tidy up his room today he became really obstinate and shouted at her, 'No, you clear up.' When she replied that she had no intention of doing so, he replied, 'Then Claudia [his sister] can do it.'

The little girl makes a connection between being good, clearing up and herself; the little boy rejects any such connection and delegates it to women instead – he doesn't think of his father in this connection. Of course, later on I will have enough trouble with Anneli refusing to tidy up, but the starting point is basically quite different for the two children.

Schorschi's sitting on my lap and we're leafing through a newspaper. There's a large advertisement showing a woman gazing out, helpless and seductive. Schorschi points to it, saying, 'You're only a woman and I'm a man.'

22 August 1984 (3 years)

Anneli and I are driving into Munich. Everything is very quiet. Suddenly, without any warning, Anneli asks, 'I am a boy, aren't I, Mummy?'

I'm taken aback and reply, 'Why do you want to know?'

Anneli: "Cos Schorschi keeps saying, "You're just a girl and I'm a boy." But I'm a boy, too, aren't I, Mummy?'

She asks in such a heart-rending and urgent manner that I just say 'yes'. The problem has obviously been occupying her for some time. I was too surprised to be able to explain it all to her there and then in the car and so released her with a yes.

29 August 1984 (3 years)

I'm telling Anneli and Schorschi a story about a mole called Grabowski and when I get to the bit where the meadow is measured I lower my voice. I speak more slowly and clearly – everything in my manner indicates something of particular importance. I say, 'And then the men came and measured everything and built houses.' The children understand the message: men – build houses – equals important.

30 August 1984 (3 years)

Anneli and I are with Schorschi and Christa. Schorschi is grizzling today and being aggressive towards Anneli. Christa doesn't react passively towards their squabbling as many boys' mothers do, leaving them to sort it out themselves, but gives Anneli verbal support in her attempts to parry Schorschi by distancing herself from his behaviour and thus isolating him. Maybe her son's getting on her nerves today. In spirit I'm also on Anneli's side.

Anneli gazes at Christa and I can see how eagerly she responds to her encouraging glances. Casting aside all uncertainty she puts a conviction and determination into her scolding and shoving we haven't seen before. Schorschi withdraws, as Anneli was previously wont to do. He sulks and says Anneli is stupid. I'm surprised at just how much influence a different attitude has on the behaviour of the children and how quickly Anneli's self-confidence is increased because she feels support. Of course, what I'm saying is obvious, but I'm sure nobody thinks of it when they're saying girls are naturally shy and reserved. Today we were openly disapproving of *his* behaviour. He no longer represented the norm Anneli had to adjust to (hit him back, don't be frightened, keep tight hold of it, etc.); instead, she was the norm and the result was quite a change in her behaviour.

2 September 1984 (3 years 1 month)
Anneli is very interested when I tell her I'll be going back to work soon and that she's going to go to kindergarten. On her way to bed she asks, 'It's not real work, is it, Mummy, like men do, but just a teeny weeny bit of work?'

9 September 1984 (3 years 1 month)
We're walking in Switzerland with Christa, Schorschi, his father and the woman who will be running the kindergarten and who has joined us so that the children can get used to her a bit.*

The two children have big sticks and are pretending to ride motorbikes. One of them has broken down and has to be repaired, so they do the repairs with imaginary tools of twigs they find. Schorschi has got a knife, and Anneli a screwdriver, since 'you can't repair a motorbike with a knife', which is true enough. In this case the boy was not being the more competent. But no one pays any attention to that. Anyway, Anneli gets up from her work, after many 'phut phuts' and 'brrms' and announces that the repairs are finished and that we can now move on. The adults are about to move off when Schorschi shouts, 'No! It's not ready yet.' Where-upon all the adults stop again and watch Schorschi. About fifteen seconds later he gets up, saying, 'Now it's finished,' and we all

---

*Marianne and some of her friends and neighbours had organised the setting up of a new playgroup in their area, to which both Anneli and Schorschi were to go. (*Translator's note.*)

walk on. Although objectively he has shown himself to be less competent with his choice of tool, his decision about the repair's completion is taken as the correct one, thus signalling to Anneli that what she says is unimportant.

Ten minutes later the motorbikes have broken down again. Schorschi looks for a stick on his own, but Anneli doesn't join in. We ask her why. She answers, 'I'm not a repair man.' When asked why, she says, 'I don't know' and just stands there sadly. We persuade her to get a tool and she pokes around until Schorschi gives the order to move on. Once again we all obey him. It doesn't occur to anyone to ask Anneli what she thinks – whether she believes they have completed the repair. In fact she was still busy, but no one pays her any attention – just the opposite to what had previously happened with Schorschi.

Women's interest in technology is spoiled very early and dominance given to little men.

10 September 1984 (3 years 1 month)
This afternoon Schorschi is a bit tired, or perhaps he's having a bad day, in any case he manages to hit or bump into Anneli while they're playing with the various bits of wood they've been dragging around with them, thus hurting her. Anneli, who is no longer at her best, either, bursts into tears and assumes he's doing it deliberately. Schorschi's father makes fun of her for crying and puts her in her place. We three women look on without saying a word. Not a word to Schorschi to be more careful or to stop messing around with such large sticks.

So once again the girl is put under pressure for reacting the way she does, even though the boy is the cause of it. She isn't to cry when he hurts her. Nor does he have to stop hurting her.

11 September 1984 (3 years 1 month)
Anneli asks me while we're out walking, 'Do I look like a cheeky lad, Mummy, with my hair so short?'

Me: 'You're a cheeky lass.'

Anneli won't accept cheeky lass, but insists on lad. An hour later she looks at her reflection in my sunglasses and asks anxiously, 'My hair's still short, isn't it?'

Me: 'Why?'

She: ''Cos then I'm a cheeky lad.'

12 September 1984 (3 years 1 month)

It's time the children were going to bed. Anneli and Schorschi get undressed. Schorschi leaves his clothes on the floor. When his father points this out to him Schorschi gets hold of his clothes, carries them into the kitchen, throws them at Christa's feet and says, 'You clear up, not me.'

13 September 1984 (3 years 1 month)

We're out walking again. Anneli announces that she has to pee, whereupon Schorschi says he has to as well. Anneli crouches down and so does Schorschi. Then Christa goes up to him, giggles and bursts out laughing. She draws the attention of the other adults to the way he pees. Schorschi's father roars with laughter. Then Christa takes hold of Schorschi, carries him about five metres away from where he was, puts him on the edge of the ravine and says, 'Look, now you can pee right down in there. Come on, take out your willie.' Schorschi does so and is praised by both his parents. Both stand next to him, saying how wonderful his willie is and how marvellously he can pee.

Anneli stands watching. Nobody admires the way she does a weewee. With her it seems to be just a normal bodily function. The rest of the day she insists on running round without her knickers on and every time she pees she sticks her tummy out and tries to produce a particularly long flow.

As we are climbing down the hill, the children are playing 'lock up'. Anneli gets tight hold of my hand and says, 'Now I'll put chains on you and hang you up.'

Me: 'Why?'

Anneli: 'Because you're a woman.'

So I wasn't imagining it; the poster of the chained woman we saw a few weeks ago has had its effect on her. What effect does it have on little boys?

16 September 1984 (3 years 1 month)

While we're out on a ramble we come to a small fence. Anneli I know will dash straight up to it, scramble on to it and start doing gymnastics. Then Schorschi sees it and wants to do the same. He also runs up to it, pushes her out of the way and climbs over. Anneli stands and watches. When he's over she follows. No one tells Schorschi he ought to let Anneli over first. Christa and I stand nearby discussing how dependent Schorschi is on Anneli's ideas and that there is a danger of his simply copying her and not developing ideas of his own. Christa thinks this might be prejudicial to his own personal development.

We don't discuss the problem of the boy taking over the girl's idea, making it his own and putting it into practice, pushing her aside. We don't bother about how the girl's personality may be damaged by this, that as her idea becomes fact she is supplanted by him and has to watch on as he 'acts' first.

Isn't this like those mixed-sex conversations in which a thought or idea expressed by a woman is ignored until it is taken up and put forward by a man, then finding general acclaim?[45] Girls learn early that it's not up to them to put their thoughts and ideas into practice, but that they are expected only to imitate, and that it is boys who act.

Isn't that our 'innate' feminine passivity?

17 September 1984 (3 years 1 month)
We're walking beside a little lake when we encounter a woman with a baby in a pram and a boy of about three pulling a boat along in the water. I draw Anneli's attention to them. 'Ooh look, Anneli, there's a little baby. Go and look at it.' Somehow I don't say, 'Look, Anneli, there's a little boat, go across and play with it.' We all know that women naturally attach more importance to personal relationships.

At home Anneli insists on ringing Martin (aged five). I dial, hear the receiver being picked up at the other end, and then nothing but breathing. No name, no hello – nothing. I assume that this is Martin and ask him to give me his mother. One final breath and then I hear Ellen. She immediately apologises for Martin, saying, 'He just can't manage any of those conversational phrases; his manner is typically masculine, he only says what's absolutely necessary. Not like women and girls who can go chattering on, he's a real man.' As far as I could tell he was just awkward – but, of course, whatever men do, it's not judged negatively.

In the evening there is a meeting of the parents to discuss the

*girl can be a boy OK
but not other way round*

start of the playgroup. The supervisor explains that when the four children are playing together (three girls and one boy) Schorschi is sometimes on the defensive, he also wants to be a girl and insists that he is able to have a baby. A look of horror appears on the face of one of the mothers. She maintains that this could have a traumatic effect on Schorschi's development and lead to identity crises.

If a girl wants to be a boy adults react differently. They laugh, as for example when we were in the South Tyrol and the girls felt like boys with their short hair. That's amusing and no one worries about their identity problems as women.

18 September 1984 (3 years 1 month)
Anneli notices the sleeve of an album of classical music lying around. She asks, 'Does that man play the music?' pointing to the picture. I answer yes. At the same time I suddenly remember the situation a year ago (20 November 1983) when I failed to grasp why Anneli assumed that making music was a male prerogative. Now it's quite clear to me. I look through our records and discover that of 95 sleeves only three show the picture of a woman; two of these are classical paintings of women, the third is a doll. The other pictures are of landscapes, towns, musical instruments and, over and over again, men, groups, quartets, orchestras, great masters. It's quite clear that music is made by men. The sleeves of light music are not much better. They only depict a woman if she is the star.

Anneli has said a few times quite unexpectedly, 'Mummy, I don't tickle my mary ann any more.'

I ask her why not.

Anneli: 'Because Schorschi doesn't.'

Me: 'But he hasn't got a mary ann to tickle.'

Anneli: 'Why has he only got a willie?'

Me: 'Because he's a boy.'

Whereupon Anneli says in a regretful, disappointed, sympathetic tone, 'But it doesn't matter, does it, Mummy, that he hasn't got a mary ann?' And you can tell from her tone of voice that she means she likes him just the same.

19 September 1984 (3 years 1 month)
Anneli and Schorschi are playing and running around the house

half naked. In the afternoon a joint outing of the playgroup is planned for the children with their parents. So they have to get dressed. Anneli announces that she wants to wear her skirt. That's okay by me and she fetches it from the chest of drawers in her room.

Schorschi stands at the bottom of the stairs and announces loud and clear that he wants to wear a skirt as well. I ignore him and go into the kitchen to see to something. He follows me, stands in front of me and repeats his request. Of course, I don't say no, but try to put him off by offering him something to eat. He responds and eats it. I'm just beginning to feel relieved and am thinking how cleverly I've got out of this predicament when he starts again with demands for a skirt. I'm reluctant and detect in myself a tremendous resistance to fulfilling what is in itself a perfectly harmless wish. He is, after all, the only boy among four girls, and to top it all the playgroup leader, who is normally in trousers, was also wearing a skirt this morning. His wish thus seems to me to be stimulated not by any deep seated psychic disorder but simply by the desire to imitate.

However, I pretend not to hear him and leave the room without answering. I feel really annoyed that I can't just put him into a skirt and forget about it. But I can't and find myself frantically looking for excuses. And then, thanks goodness, the obvious one occurs to me – that we haven't got another skirt, as Anneli only possesses one. This doesn't satisfy Schorschi. And now he starts to wail in earnest. Suddenly I remember that Anneli's old skirt is somewhere down in the cellar. Even so, I still have enormous inhibitions about putting it on Schorschi. It seems to me as though it is violating the child and I'm worried about what Christa might say.

But while I'm dressing Schorschi all the time I'm thinking, 'Thank goodness it's Christa, she'll understand; she's bound to go along with it and not laugh at him or make a fuss.' Nevertheless I feel as though I'm desecrating some particularly sacred treasure and it's only because I know Christa that I can risk it. I would never have dared to fulfil the child's wishes in the case of any other mother I know in Munich. So Schorschi gets his skirt and hops around in great glee.

The playgroup assembles. None of the children pays any attention at all to Schorschi. And Christa also guesses what's up when she sees him and says nothing. One mother wears an expression of some amazement and the other adults cannot resist making little jokes and other comments, with a degree of contempt about the 'attire' which varies according to the speaker.

Now it's clear enough why boys despise and ridicule everything they connect with girls. Since they are not allowed to act like them their only escape is into the supposedly more positive manliness. And, secondly, the comments and example of adults show them that what is not acceptable for them is in itself contemptible. Pity! I think they're missing something.

20 September 1984 (3 years 1 month)
After a very pleasant day out with friends we go into a restaurant for a meal. Anneli and I sit down together on a bench. She clambers up the back of the bench on to a jutting wall and kneeling there can see through a window into the kitchen.

While we're ordering and talking Anneli is occupied clambering up and down. She particularly enjoys smiling at the kitchen staff. The manageress comes and says, 'Laddie, you're really enjoying yourself climbing up and down there, aren't you?'

Anneli looks annoyed and says, 'I'm a girl.'

The manageress says, 'And I thought you was a boy, 'cos you're so good at climbing.'

Another customer intervenes, 'No, she's a girl and that's why she's interested in the kitchen.'

21 September 1984 (3 years 1 month)
Anneli and I are driving into town to pick Klaus up at the office. We park in the office car park and have to show our permit. Anneli wants me to read out what is on it, so I read, 'This car belongs to Klaus.'

She replies indignantly, 'No, Mummy, that's not true. The car belongs to us; you, me and Daddy, not just Daddy.' That was pretty stupid of me. Thank goodness things are changing. I was glad she put me right.

She's been saying after dinner lately, according to who has done the cooking, 'Daddy (or Mummy), that was a nice meal.' And Daddy is as often praised as I am. Anneli is learning to take for granted, unlike me as a child, that men can cook.

In the evening she's playing at clowns and chants, 'Hocus pocus fidibus, abracadabra simsabus, three times black for Lady Puss.' I'm pleased that feminine forms occur to her as readily as do masculine ones. I begin to believe that it is possible to change something, albeit not very much, through education. A gleam of hope for the future.

January 1985 (3 years 5 months)

I am now once again completely taken up with my working day and am separated from Anneli from 7.30 in the morning until 5 in the evening.

I had been intending to continue the diary both for myself and for Anneli's sake, but my entries are growing rarer. I haven't got anything to write about because nothing occurs to me any more. I don't really register the comments any more, make the connections or try to understand everything. There are no more stories about learning to be a girl. Has the world changed so much that all the things I noted in previous years are now over now I'm back at work?

There's only one answer to that: now that I'm so terribly busy and continually under pressure I no longer have the same degree of sensitivity and receptivity for Anneli's life and experiences. Many of these, of course, I miss during the hours we are apart; some I miss because I don't recognise the connections; some I don't listen to in quite the same way, now that my mind is geared to work. And finally, at night, when everything else has been attended to, I'm simply too tired to think clearly, to remember the events of the day and write them down.

Perhaps the much-despised housewives – discredited sometimes even among feminists – need to be more conscious of the power their way of life contains, of the processsess of recognition they gain and can develop. All the things I became aware of and the conclusions I came to would have been impossible if I had not spent the first three years of Anneli's life being a 'housewife'.

Notes

1   Margaret Mead, 1949, p 81ff.
2   S. and J. Condry, *Sex Differences. A Study of the Eye of the Beholder*, quoted in Senta Trömel-Plötz, 1984.

3   Simone de Beauvoir, 1983, p 309.
4   Ibid.
5   Carol Hagemann-White, 1984, p 84ff.
6   Elena Gianini Belotti, 1975, p 76.
7   Ibid, p 60.
8   Ibid, p 60.
9   Ibid, p 72.
10 ·Helene Deutsch, 1944, p 226 (note 5).
11 Simone de Beauvoir, 1983, p 299.
12 D. W. Winnicott, *The Child, the Family and the Outside World*, quoted in Badinter, 1982, p 255 and p 259.
13 Bundestag, *6th Youth Report*, 1984, p 31.
14 Ursula Scheu, 1981, p 79; Carol Hagemann-White, 1984, p 59.
15 Bundestag, *6th Youth Report*, 1984, p 32.
16 Cynthia Cockburn, April 1984.
17 Quoted in Shulamith Firestone, 1979, p 68.
18 cf. Cynthia Cockburn, April 1984.
19 Marianne Wex, 1980; Senta Trömel-Plötz, 1984.
20 Mary Daly, 1979, p 199.
21 George Orwell, 1949, p 147.
22 Luise Pusch, 1983, p 370.
23 cf. Astrid Matthiae, 1986.
24 Ibid.
25 Bundestag, *6th Youth Report*, 1984, p 33.
26 Shulamith Firestone, 1979, pp 48 and 77.
27 Phyllis Chesler, 1972.
28 Margaret Mead, quoted in Kate Millett, 1977, p 224, note 215.
29 Margaret Mead, 1949, p 158
30 cf. Elizabeth Gould Davis, 1973; Ernest Bornemann, 1975.
31 Senta Trömel-Plötz, 1984, p 20ff.
32 Ibid, p 340
33 cf. Kate Millett, 1977, p 181; Simone de Beauvoir, 1983, p 300.
34 Sigmund Freud, 1964, p 132.
35 Cynthia Cockburn, April 1984, p 203.
36 Schmidt, et al., 1973; cf. also Kate Millett, 1977.
37 cf. Marianne Wex, 1980, 18ff.
38 J. J. Rousseau, 1974, p 333.
39 cf. Ursula Scheu, 1981, p 98.
40 cf. Imme de Haen, 1984.
41 cf. Ursula Scheu, 1981, p 89.
42 Simone de Beauvoir, 1983, p 300.
43 How do the gentlemen ride? – trapp, trapp; And the farmers? – stupp, stupp; And the noblemen? – gallop, gallop; And the ladies and maidens? – down they tumble into the ditch.
44 Kate Millett, 1977, p 36.
45 cf. Ursula Scheu, 1981, p 79.

Afterword

> Even if my mother's diary sometimes gives you the feeling that her methods of bringing me up in a different way failed, *I* think the end-result was a success!
>
> *Annemarie,* aged 13 years*

Thirteen years ago, I began my experiment to try to raise my daughter in an atmosphere free from the stereotypical gender roles which are forced upon us in this male-dominated society. I was well-aware that my experiment could only work if political change in favour of women's rights accompanied my efforts. I also knew that I could not work miracles alone, that I could not single-handedly alter my daughter's future. Nor did I wish to raise her in an over-protective feminist milieu. I felt that it was far more important to combine normal day-to-day life with hope for a better future for women and men. I was convinced that a child's growth was not simply dependent on the kind of home environment which that child's parent(s) provided. Rather, the everyday behaviour exhibited by all women and men ultimately makes a lasting impression on all our children. The example that I set for my daughter would indeed need to be confirmed and mirrored consistently so that it would appear to be the norm into which she would naturally and easily grow.

Annemarie is now $13\frac{1}{2}$ years old. Up to now, I can truly say that I am satisfied with the fruits of my labour. The results are very much in keeping with my original expectations and hopes. My daughter's behaviour is different from that of other girls in many

*'Anneli' was the name she used when she was very young, and unable to say 'Annemarie'. (*Publisher's note.*)

ways. She possesses a great deal of inner independence which can easily be seen in the straightforward way she goes about achieving her goals. Annemarie does not wait passively for other people to make decisions or take action, rather, she takes matters into her own hands, at least as far as a child of her age can. When in doubt she simply asks me for help. Yet if she notices that her plan does not truly meet her needs, she can, at any time, move on. For example, she was not baptised as a baby. At the age of ten, when all of her classmates were preparing for their First Communion, Annemarie decided that she would like to be baptised. She then made all of the necessary arrangements to attend religious lessons. During one of the classes, the priest compared God to a father who concerns himself with the welfare of his family, protecting the mother and children from harm so that they feel safe and secure. Annemarie felt compelled to disagree, as she herself had seen so many families – including her own – that had split up through the father's fault. She had also seen how mothers and children had then gone on to lead fulfilled lives without the presence of a father. She told her stories in class to substantiate her argument. When the priest replied that she was a 'poor child', she found his comment discriminatory and no longer wished to join the church. No priest's authority, no celebration, no pretty dress and no gifts could tempt her to go along with something that was so alien to her own under-standing of reality. Annemarie had grown up in an atmosphere where women's roles were different. She saw being a single mother as something positive, not disadvantageous. This enabled her to walk away from a situation which she found did not fit her needs.

Annemarie: My mother never forced me into any sort of 'role'. Neither the role of 'being a boy' nor of 'being a girl'. But even though my mother never did this, I had a lot of pressure from children at school or friends, from adults and relatives. Maybe it was the way I was brought up, maybe it was in my nature that I had a strong will which made me be what *I* wanted to be, and not what others thought would be suitable for a girl.

At times, she has faced contradictions, difficulties and even isolation because of the way in which she was raised. It is in these moments that I have truly wondered how much can my child's spirit take? I have always had to weigh the personal strength of my daughter against my own political, perhaps utopian, vision. This has sometimes led us to conform to prescribed gender roles, a source of amusement, both at the time and afterwards. I am reminded of a visit to the beach, when Annemarie, in order to compete with the other 'beach beauties', sat through a three-hour procedure in which she had her long, thick, blond hair braided into 33 individual braids! But generally, she dresses appropriately and does not restrict herself to always wearing trousers or dressing like a boy. As long as a certain way of dress seems practical and comfortable, she follows the trend. She draws the line, however, when she experiences peer pressure from other girls. She loves to cook and create a pleasant atmosphere when entertaining friends at our house. Without a doubt, she has many 'feminine' characteristics and genuinely enjoys having them. But this does not keep her from exhibiting 'other' characteristics. Thus, she does not let any of her numerous skills go to waste.

Once, when she was 11 years old, I heard her hammering away in her room. When I went to see what the commotion was, I saw that she had dismantled her chest of drawers and rebuilt it, in its entirety, in another corner of her room. Obviously, she has a way with tools. She also has a knack when it comes to the many repairs that need to be done around the house. In situations where I would most likely call a handyman, or handywoman for that matter, she has a ball trying to do the repairs herself. She even designed and built her rabbit's cage.

After I had finished the journal, Annemarie attended kindergarten for four years. Whenever any of the boys in kindergarten wanted to 'take away' her toys through brute force, Annmarie's reaction was very direct. She always chose not to hit back right away. Instead, she said 'No!' in a manner that was loud and clear. If the boys didn't get the message, they were given a second warning, 'If a girl says no, then she means no!' Then and only then did she hit back. Through such experiences my daughter has learned to take her own 'yeses' and 'noes' seriously and to always 'stick to her guns'. Unfortunately, very few kindergarten teachers were supportive of Annemarie or any other girl who defended herself. In this case, sadly, Annemarie's upbringing did not find corresponding support from the outside world. Yet, I always tried to validate her feelings that her actions were just.

She then began primary school at the age of seven. Her first day was similarly difficult. One of the boys tore her beloved fox tail off her school-bag and commenced to destroy it. He also declared 'Look, she's got a prick,* she thinks she's a boy.' Her feelings as the underdog in this situation were confirmed by the fact that the school authorities were clearly reluctant to come to her defence. This caused her great anxiety for quite some time during her daily walks to school. Because of her fear, she chose to take a lengthy detour. Through this experience she learned to evaluate the degree of danger in a situation and to retreat when necessary. She also realised that as long as one remains helpless, one will continue to be afraid. Annemarie decided to do something to change her situation. As her school years progressed she learned to fight back. She took judo classes in which she was one of only four girls in a class with 42 boys. One day, Annemarie was defending herself from one of the boys, using punches and kicks learnt in judo class. When the boy began to cry, the teacher told him, 'That's what you get when you pick a fight with a girl.' At long last, Annemarie felt that her capabilities had been acknowledged and she had been treated equally. In this instance, the teacher had echoed her upbringing. From that point on, Annemarie was noticeably more self-determined in the case of an attack at school. She was even able to get a few of her girlfriends to defend themselves when they were being attacked.

When Annemarie was six her father and I split up, and since then she and I have been on our own. I continued to work full time. Several different babysitters looked after her in the afternoon, because in Germany the children come home from school at 1 p.m.

Annemarie has an independent, career-oriented mother who offers her financial security, without being economically dependent on her father. As might be expected, she also experiences the drawbacks of such a lifestyle: hard work, discipline, and a lack of free time. She has met numerous colleagues of mine, who are women in high-ranking positions, as well as politicians. All this has

*The word used here is '*Schwanz*', which can mean either tail or penis. This word-play is much more effective and common in German. (*Translator's note.*)

shaped the expectations she has for her own future. This, I believe, gives me the realistic hope that she will be able to reach for the stars when searching for her own career, just as I have always wished for her, since long before her birth.

The last 20 years of political change, sparked by the women's movement have resulted in more equal rights and better career opportunities for women, though we have often felt that these changes have not been rapid or wide-ranging enough. Nonetheless, they have clearly had a marked influence on our daughters' career plans.

Annemarie does not worry about choosing between a career and children. She wants both. When she begins to consider a particular career, she poses adequate and well-thought-out questions about educational training, qualifications and the secrets to success. However, she is not concerned about managing both career and 'family responsibilities'. After listening to my answers she evaluates the situation and decides whether she wishes to continue to pursue a dream career or not. She is well-aware that the development of any career involves many, tiny, laborious steps. She has had the chance to observe her mother, as well as many other women, go through the process. Through my experiences with my daughter, I have come to realise that women have now established a tradition of passing 'insider' career information from one generation to another. This practice used to be for fathers and sons only.

I do not intend to say that other girls do not have equally exciting career goals. Claudia would like to be a famous journalist and Sandra would like to be Chief Constable. Yet, neither of them have any idea as to how to go about accomplishing their goals or how to achieve such success. When I start to tell them what all this entails their mothers object, saying that I shouldn't burst their daughters' bubbles, or that this too shall pass as soon as they find a boyfriend. And indeed, it all too often does.

Are these mothers unable to be supportive of their daughters' plans because they themselves have had so little work experience? I am convinced that in future generations, as more and more women enter the employment market and also obtain better positions within that market, this will inevitably change. Girls will not only dream about careers, they will also be able to plan them, turning their dreams into reality.

At 12, Annemarie was already planning her future. As part of this plan she decided that in order to fully learn the English language she should attend a school in Great Britain. She has been studying there for one and a half years now, at a girls' school, and the differences have surprised her.

Annemarie: I had problems putting up with the girls *and* boys in my old school in Germany, which was a mixed school. The girls and boys were typical examples of children, brought up in the old tradition of 'boys are strong and brave' and 'girls are sweet and weak'. The girls worshipped the boys, and the boys looked down on them. There were 12 boys and 16 girls in my class, but the boys were so noisy and dominant, that it seemed like there were 20 boys and only a few girls. Now I'm at an English girls' school, things have changed quite a lot. Suddenly I notice that girls can be noisy too, that girls can put up their hands to answer a question without blushing, and that girls can even speak up while reading aloud without being asked to by the teacher. Now I have some girlfriends who think the same way as me. Maybe there were girls thinking the same way as me in the mixed school too, maybe they just didn't dare show it.

As a result of her upbringing, Annemarie has the capacity to see everyday occurrences with more insight than most children. She is also able to evaluate these carefully and effectively.

Annemarie: I notice things I couldn't talk about with my friends, because it is perfectly normal for them. For example, when I am at my friends' homes and it is the kind of family where the father goes to work all day and the mother doesn't work at all, or only part-time, so she can be there for the children, I sometimes have supper with them. And when it comes to who gets what, the father usually gets the best, the biggest, and sometimes a different meal from all the others. I think this is very unfair, because we work all day too, and yet he is considered as more important. Another example is a friend of mine who never tells me, when we talk about vacations, how she feels about where she's been. She just tells me what her dad felt, and said, and did. When I notice things like that I feel really annoyed!

All in all, our life together can be compared to a hike in the mountains, always a steady uphill climb. The paths to the top are often arduous and rocky. Now and again, we find ourselves surrounded by beauty and peace. Then we sit and rest for a while. With this combination of uphill climbs and peaceful rests, I hope to continue to eliminate some of the barriers that might otherwise limit my daughter's role as a woman in our society.

References

Badinter, Elisabeth, *The Myth of Motherhood*, Souvenir Press, London, 1982.

de Beauvoir, Simone, *The Second Sex*, Penguin, Harmondsworth, 1983.

Belotti, Elena Gianini, *Little Girls. Social Conditioning and its Effects on the Stereotyped Role of Women During Infancy*, translated and produced collectively by Lisa Appignanesi, Amelia Fletcher, Toschiko Schimura, Sian Williams and Jean Wordsworth, Writers and Readers Co-operative, London, 1975.

Bornemann, Ernest, *Das Patriarchat* (*Patriarchy*), Fischer, Frankfurt am Main, 1975.

Bundestag, *6th Youth Report: Bericht der Sachverständigen-kommission zur Chancengleichheit der Mädchen in der BRD* (*Official Committee's Report on Equality of Opportunity for Girls in the Federal German Republic*), Dt. Bundestag, 10 WP, Dr. 100/1007, 1984.

Chesler, Phyllis, *Women and Madness*, Allen Lane, London, 1972.

Cockburn, Cynthia, 'Weibliche Aneignung in der Technik' ('Female adaptation to technology'), in *Das Argument* no. 144, April 1984.

Daly, Mary, *Gyr./Ecology*, The Women's Press, London 1979.

Gould Davis, Elizabeth, *The First Sex*, Dent, London, 1973.

Deutsch, Helene, *The Psychology of Women*, Grune & Stratton, New York, 1944.

Erler, Gisela Anna, 'Die weibliche Wende. Argument gegen die Selbst-verstümmelung' ('The female turning point, arguments against self-mutilation'), article in *Freibeuter*, Berlin, 1983.

Firestone, Shulamith, *The Dialectic of Sex: The Case for Feminist*

Revolution, introduced by Rosalind, Delamr, The Women's Press, London, 1979.

de Haen, Imme, *Aber die Jüngste war die Allerschönste* (*But the Youngest Girl was the Prettiest of All*), Fischer, Frankfurt am Main, 1984.

Hagemann-White, Carol, *Sozialisation: Mannlich-weiblich?* (*Socialisation: Masculine-feminine?*) Leske und Budrich, Leverkusen, 1984.

Karsten, Garbriele, *Mariechens Weg ins Glück? Die Diskriminierung in Grundschullesebüchern* (*Little Mary's Path to Happiness? Discrimination in Primary School Reading Books*), Fisher, Berlin, 1977.

Kohlberg, Lawrence, *The Psychology of Moral Development*, Harper & Row, San Francisco, 1984.

Kunstmann, Antje, *Frauenemanzipation und Erziehung* (*Women's Emancipation and Education*), Raith Verlag, Starnberg, 1971.

Marrhiae, Astrid, *Von pfiffigen Peter und der faden Anna* (*Of Bright Peter and Dull Anna*), Fischer, Frankfurt am Main, 1986.

Mead, Margaret, *Male and Female*, Victor Gollancz, London, 1949.

Millett, Kate, *Sexual Politics*, Virago, London, 1977.

Mussen, P. H., 'Geschlechtsrollenentwicklung in früher Kindheit' ('Sex-role development in early childhood') in Gotz/Kaltschmid, *Sozialisation und Erziehung* (*Socialisation and Education*), Darmstadt, 1978.

Orwell, George, *1984*, Twentieth Century Texts, London, 1949.

Preissing, Christa and Best, Edetraud, 'Zum Umgang mit Mädchen in Kinderstätten unter besonderer Berücksichtigung der 3–6 jährigen' ('Dealing with girls in child care centres, with special reference to 3–6-year-olds') in *6th Youth Report*, 1984.

Pusch, Luise (ed.), *Feminismus, Inspektion der Herrenkultur* (*Feminism, Examining Gentlemen's Culture*), Frankfurt am Main, 1983.

Rousseau, J. J., *Emile*, translated by Barbara Foxley, Dent, London, 1974.

Scheu, Ursula, *Wir werden nicht als Mädchen geboren – wir*

werden dazu gemacht (*We Are Not Born Girls, We Are Made Into Them*), Fischer, Frankfurt an Main, 1981.

Schmidt, *et al, Frauenfeindlichkeit* (*Misogyny*), Munich, 1973.

Schultz, Dagmar, *Ein Mächen ist fast so gut wie ein Junge* (*A Girl is Almost as Good as a Boy*, Frauenselbsteurlag, Berlin, 1980.

Sichermann, Barbara, 'Zur Politick des Weiblichen' ('On the politics of the feminine') in *6th Youth Report*, 1984.

Trömel Plötz, Senta, *Frauensprache – Sprache der Veränderung* (*Women's Language – Language of Change*), Fischer, Frankfurt am Main, 1982.

Trömel-Plötz, Senta, *Gewalt durch Sprache* (*Violence Through Language*), Fischer, Frankfurt am Main, 1984.

Wex, Marianne, *'Weibliche' und 'männliche' Körpersprache* (*'Male' and 'Female' Body Language*), self-published, Frankfurt, 1980.

THE LIBRARY
WEST KENT COLLEGE
0075504 BROOK STREET
TONBRIDGE